A History *of* Money *and* Banking *in* Barbados

A History of Money and Banking in Barbados, 1627–1973

Eric ARMSTRONG

UNIVERSITY OF THE WEST INDIES PRESS

Jamaica • Barbados • Trinidad and Tobago

University of the West Indies Press
7A Gibraltar Hall Road   Mona
Kingston 7   Jamaica
www.uwipress.com

© 2010 by Eric Armstrong

All rights reserved. Published 2010

CATALOGUING-IN-PUBLICATION DATA

Armstrong, Eric.

A history of money and banking in Barbados, 1627–1973 / Eric Armstrong.

p. cm.

Includes bibliographical references.

ISBN: 978-976-640-239-6

1. Money – Barbados – History. 2. Banks and banking – Barbados – History. I. Title.
HG792.5.A84 2010   332.0972′9

Set in Stone Serif 9/14 x 27

Book and cover design by Robert Harris.

Printed in the United States of America.

Contents

Foreword / **vii**

Preface and Acknowledgements / **xi**

1   The Early Currency System / **1**

2   The Introduction of British Coins / **16**

3   The Advent of the Banks / **38**

4   Metallic Currency, 1850–1947 / **55**

5   The Expansion of Banks and Paper Currency / **75**

6   West Indian Currency Unification / **102**

     Appendix 1:   Imports and Exports / **125**

     Appendix 2:   Exports of Sugar and Molasses / **126**

     Appendix 3:   Banking Regulations / **127**

     Notes / **131**

     Selected Bibliography / **147**

     Index / **149**

Foreword

KEITH HUNTE

THIS STUDY IS A most welcome addition to the all-too-limited historical literature on money and banking in Barbados and the English-speaking Caribbean. The author is an economist who has had a distinguished career as a practitioner and as a teacher. This book fills a critical gap in our knowledge of the experience of Barbados and other former English colonies in the Caribbean as they sought, over three centuries, to develop or have access to an appropriate medium of exchange and commercial banking services.

Eric Armstrong has completed a labour of love. Over several years, and even when he was in full-time employment as an economist, he would seize every available opportunity to track down relevant documents focusing mainly on repositories in Barbados, the United Kingdom and Jamaica.

Through painstaking research, and guided by his professional insights into the respective roles of money and banking within an economy, he has produced a book that will have strong appeal for teachers, students and a reading public that wishes to satisfy its curiosity about the antecedents of the Barbadian economy, the Central Bank of Barbados and the several commercial banks that are now conspicuous features of the financial landscape.

The study reminds us that the colonial history of Barbados and other Caribbean territories is interwoven with the story of the birth and development of European capitalism. The Barbadian planters, artisans and other workers (both free and unfree) of the seventeenth and eighteenth centuries were operating in local, regional and transatlantic markets in circumstances where they were relatively powerless and unable to induce change in the rules that sought to determine the official medium of exchange for transactions conducted in Barbados. Indeed, the policymakers themselves were not too well informed about the true sources of wealth and the interrelationship between money supply and the accumulation of wealth. John Kenneth Galbraith, in his informative book *Money: Whence It Came, Where It Went*, indicates that for the greater part of what is described as the modern era, policymakers operated on assumptions, several of which were unsound and/or misleading. In response to the petitions of the colonists, the policymakers in England based their decisions on their perceptions of the way in which the imperial interests would be affected by any action that might, on the surface, appear to be an appropriate response to the issues raised by the petitioners. In addition, their mindset was formed by the conventional wisdom of the time about money, trade and capital formation. The publication of Adam Smith's *Wealth of Nations* was one of the first efforts to successfully challenge some of these assumptions and lay the foundation for the discipline of economics.

It is against this background that the recurrent attempts by interest groups in Barbados to have a reliable medium of exchange and one that favoured their situation and their economic interests – among which was an attempt to establish and operate a bank – are described. These accounts provide a further illustration of the colonial predicament.

The late eighteenth and the early nineteenth centuries witnessed a series of events that prompted significant changes in official policy with regard to money and banking in colonial Barbados. The intensification of imperial rivalry and wars culminating in the Napoleonic War led to a substantial increase in the number of British troops stationed in the Caribbean, including Barbados. The provision of a regular stipend for these men required an outflow of funds from Britain to Barbados. Second, the dismantling of the institution of slavery and its replacement by the apprenticeship system and ultimately by a wage-labour system necessitated the provision of an appropriate money supply to support the system. These factors, among others, produced important changes in policy with regard to establishing what currency would be legal tender. Correspondingly, the expansion of the sugar industry in the newly acquired colonies of Trinidad and British Guiana attracted substantial investment to the region. The establishment of the Colonial Bank in the Caribbean in 1836 is an early manifestation of what has become axiomatic; namely, that banks follow the money trail.

In documenting the story of the early commercial banks in Barbados, the author provides good historical data that will support and encourage further investigations that should tell us a lot more about the operation of these first banks. The arrival of the Canadian banks at the turn of the century correspondingly reflected the increased interest of Canada's mercantile and financial institutions in consolidating and expanding trade with the West Indies. It should not be considered a coincidence that the inflow of remittances to Barbados at this time was making a significant impact on the level of accumulation of domestic savings.

Further, the study sheds valuable light on the background to the relatively successful efforts at regional cooperation towards the establishment of a common currency at the sub-regional level. The establishment of the British Caribbean Territories (Eastern) Board and later the establishment of the East Caribbean Currency Authority, of which Barbados was a member, were important landmarks along the circuitous road towards regional integration. Finally, the author gives a historical account of the replacement of these institutions by the Central Bank of Barbados and parallel institutions in other independent territories in the region.

This book will do more than satisfy the curiosity of the general reader. It is certain to become a valuable reference work.

Preface and Acknowledgements

THE ISLAND OF BARBADOS (166 square miles) was settled by the British in 1627 and remained a British colony until 1966 when it became an independent nation. Its economy, like that of the other West Indian islands, was based on the growing of sugar cane and on the manufacture of sugar and its by-products, molasses and rum. These commodities accounted for approximately 90 per cent of domestic exports until the 1950s when the government offered concessions to local and foreign entrepreneurs in order to diversify the economy, especially in the manufacturing and tourism sectors. (See appendices 1 and 2.)

The study of money and banking in the West Indies has been largely neglected by West Indian scholars in favour of politics and social conditions. However, within the last few years a few historians and economists have published some books and articles on this subject, but they relate mainly to Jamaica and Trinidad and Tobago. The first comprehensive study on money in the colonies was undertaken by Lord Robert Chalmers in 1893, when he wrote his monumental work *A History of Currency in the British Colonies*. In it, he devoted, inter alia, a separate chapter to each of the major British West Indian islands and British Guiana. Dr Ida Greaves in 1952 published three articles entitled "Money and Currency in Barbados" in the *Journal of the Barbados Museum and Historical Society*. These articles included some of the ground covered by Lord Chalmers in his chapter on Barbados but also other developments on the subject up to

1951. However, these two studies concentrated on the history of money and only briefly mentioned the Colonial Bank and the West India Bank; Dr Greaves did not include the advent of the Canadian banks in Barbados in the 1900s.

The aim of this book is to provide an in-depth study of money and banking in Barbados, starting from the date of the settlement in 1627 and ending with the establishment of the Central Bank of Barbados in 1973. Since the Central Bank is planning to publish a history of that institution for its first thirty years, it did not seem appropriate to preempt the intended publication. This study concentrates only on the banks that issued bank notes and not on other banks, such as the Government Agricultural Bank (later renamed the Peasants Loan Bank), the Sugar Industry Bank, the Barbados Cooperative Bank and the Government Savings Bank.

Chapter 1 deals with the coins in circulation in Barbados, from the time of settlement in 1627 to 1800; the legislation relating to barter and to metallic currency; Queen Anne's proclamation in 1704 and its effects on the economy. Chapter 2 describes the controversy in Barbados over the imperial proclamations of 1825 and 1838 relating to British silver coins and the rates given to foreign coins, that is, Spanish, Mexican, Columbian and Portuguese coins. Chapter 3 looks at the establishment of the Colonial Bank (British) in 1836 and the West India Bank, which was a West Indian bank that had its headquarters in Barbados and branches in several other islands, in 1840; the antagonism and competition between the two banks; the operation and demise of the West India Bank. Chapter 4 describes the British and foreign coins that were in circulation in the nineteenth and twentieth centuries; the policy of the British government regarding the circulation of these coins and other matters relating to seignorage and the tendering of British silver coins. Chapter 5 examines the arrival of the Canadian banks in the twentieth century; the resentment expressed by the Colonial Bank (renamed Barclays Bank, DC&O [Dominion, Colonial and Overseas] in 1925) towards the Canadian banks that were allowed to issue bank notes; banking during the war years; the introduction of Barbados government currency notes. Chapter 6 gives the background to West Indian currency unification; the Currency Conference in Barbados in 1946 and the Montego Bay Conference in 1947; the establishment, operation and demise of the British Caribbean Territories (Eastern) Group commonly called the British Caribbean Currency Board; the establishment of the East Caribbean Currency Authority.

I am indebted to Sir Keith Hunte, former principal and pro-vice chancellor of the Cave Hill campus of the University of the West Indies, and Mr Francois Jackman of the Barbados Ministry of Foreign Affairs for their comments and suggestions on the work. I am grateful to the staff of the Barbados Public Library for allowing me access to the old Barbados newspapers and to the staff of the Barbados Archives who allowed me access to the files of the Colonial Secretary's Office as well as the despatches to and from the secretary of state. I also wish to express my appreciation for the generous assistance given by the Central Bank of Barbados. This study would not have been possible if I had not been able to view the records of the Colonial Office, the Royal Mint, the Treasury and the Board of Trade at the National Archives, England. I wish to offer my sincere thanks to that institution and its staff.

I

The Early Currency System

DURING THE SEVENTEENTH and eighteenth centuries, the coins that the English settlers saw were not sterling coins but mainly Spanish coins; however, these coins were assigned values denominated in sterling and it is from this practice that the term "denominational currency" originated. During the early years of the settlement of Barbados, the currency policy of the British government was enunciated in the proclamation of James I, which stated that "the treasure of gold and silver brought into the realm should be considered as an immoveable and perpetual Stock". Similarly, a royal proclamation issued on 14 December 1661 "for the encouraging of planters in His Majesty's Island of Jamaica" stated in part that "all free persons shall have libertie without interruption, to transport themselves and their families and any [of] their goods (except onley coyne and bullion) from any our Dominions and Territories to the said Island of Jamaica".

The majority of the early colonists in the West Indies were not wealthy men, and the development of agriculture was a slow and expensive process that required external finance. The colonists exported crops to merchants in England who would then deduct from their sale the cost of the supplies advanced

1

to the planters prior to reaping, and other expenses, such as duties in England, insurance, freight and the cost of supplying the slaves. This usually resulted in an adverse balance of trade, and the colonists would invariably be indebted to these merchants. The coins in circulation in Barbados were mainly obtained from the sale of local produce to the North American colonies and from government taxes on traders, such as a levy of 20 shillings (s) imposed in 1634 on foreign ships calling at Barbados and a tax of 7 per cent on the business they transacted in the island.

In the early years, because of a shortage of currency, transactions were settled in kind using the main exports, cotton and tobacco. Since money was not plentiful, these commodities formed part, if not the whole, of the internal circulating medium and were used for the payment of goods and services as specified in legislation at that time. For example, one act stipulated that each person who was not a freeholder should pay, as tax to the governor, 20 pounds of cotton or tobacco, and another act (29 May 1644) specified that they should continue the annual payment of a pound of tobacco or cotton per acre to the governor. An act of 13 March 1648 gave church wardens the power to sell lands and so on, provided that the surveyor was paid not more than one pound of cotton for every acre surveyed. If the survey was undertaken without the governor's warrant, the surveyor would be charged 10,000 pounds of tobacco. However, from the mid 1640s, muscovado sugar replaced cotton and tobacco. In 1661, Lord Willoughby told the Council for Foreign Plantations (hereafter, the council) that sugar was the principal commodity and that some parts of Barbados afforded cotton, but the country was too barren for indigo, and ginger (at the present price) was not worth planting.[1] As a result of the dominance of sugar, payments and fines became mainly denominated in sugar (although in some instances cotton was also mentioned). For example, an act of 30 August 1656 stated that a member of the vestry who failed to attend meetings, without having an excuse, would be fined 500 pounds of muscovado sugar. Similarly, an act passed in 1656 to regulate and appoint the fees of the several officers and courts of Barbados denominated all fees in pounds of sugar. Fines were also denominated in sugar: an act of 1660 decreed that masters and overseers of families would pay a penalty of 40 pounds of sugar for not saying morning and evening prayers and a penalty of 10 pounds of cotton if a servant did not say prayers (if it was fault of master). Persons who were found in taverns, alehouses and other such establishments on a Sunday were fined 5s. A master or free man who swore, using the name of God, paid a fine of four pounds of sugar and a servant two pounds of sugar. In 1663, the treasurer was ordered to pay 150,000 pounds of sugar for the support of the government for the year.[2]

The price of sugar for paying fees and fines fluctuated over the years. An act passed on 22 November 1655 rated muscovado sugar at 3 pence (d) sterling per pound while an act passed on 29 April 1668 to reduce the interest to 10 per cent in one year stated "such money debts shall be here satisfied by muscovadoes sugar at 2d the pound (16s 8d per 100 lb)". An act of 21 October 1670 for regulating the fees payable to the secretary of Barbados rated sugar at 1s 3d for 10 pounds of sugar, that is, 12s 6d per 100 pounds. This rating remained in effect until the end of the seventeenth century. It would appear that this rating continued until the end of the seventeenth century because an act for the better regulating of outcries in open market, passed on 19 December 1688, stated that the fee of marshals for levying executions was sometimes computed in sugar, but most commonly in money, proved inconvenient, decreed that in future they should compute the money into sugar by the scale given in the act provided that the fee received in money should not exceed 12s 6d per 100 pounds.

Although fees and so on were rated in commodities, some acts passed in the early years imposed fees and the like in sterling, such as an act of 29 November 1676 "To prevent the inconvenience upon the inhabitants of this Island, by Forestallers, Ingrosses and Regrators", and an act of 12 July 1682 to pay a person 5s for killing wild monkeys and raccoons. Towards the end of the seventeenth century, currency replaced sugar as the denomination for transactions. By about 1690, the term "current money" began to appear in legislation such as in an Act passed on 8 July 1690 to grant His Excellency Colonel James Kendal a present of £1,500 current money, although some subsequent acts referred to sterling. However, from about 1704 current money became standard in legislation.

CURRENCY LEGISLATION

Legislation relating to currency in the colonies was, on occasion, made by the imperial Parliament. The usual method of legislation was by royal order in council, by proclamation, and by acts of the local legislatures, subject to the approval of the British government. During the early years of the settlement of Barbados, there was a chronic shortage of currency and several acts were passed to remedy this situation. Unfortunately, details of most of the early acts relating to metallic currency are no longer available; however, the laws compiled by Samuel Moore and those by Richard Hall give the titles of some obsolete acts enacted between 1646 and 1666. These are the act of 13 May 1646 "for the raising and advancing the value of foreign coin"; the act of 13 March 1661/2 "for the encouraging the importing of Gold and Silver into this Island"; the act of 2 July 1662 "for the repealing [of] the late Act made for advancing the value of coin"; the act of 14 April 1666 "for the advancing and raising the value of pieces of eight".

One of the early acts passed on 12 September 1651 "for the encouraging the importing of Gold and Silver into this Island" indicates the wide variety of coins that were in circulation and the rates given to each:

> English
>
> Gold – the 22 shillings piece at 29 shillings 4 pence; the 20 shillings piece at 26 shillings 8 pence and smaller pieces in proportion
>
> Silver – the 2 shillings 6 pence piece at 3 shillings 4 pence; 12 pence at 16 pence; 6 pence at 8 pence; 3 pence at 4 pence and all lesser coins in that proportion
>
> Dutch ryder in gold at 28 shillings
>
> Rix dollar (silver) at 6 shillings
>
> Crosse dollar at 5 shillings 8 pence
>
> French double pistoll at 20 shillings and the rest in proportion
>
> French crown at 9 shillings
>
> Cardecue (silver) at 2 shillings and half cardecue at 12 pence
>
> Spanish double pistoll (gold) at 20 shillings
>
> Piece of eight (silver) at 6 shillings and the lesser in proportion
>
> Portugal old testoone at 20 pence and the new testoone at 12 pence with the proviso that these coins had their just and due weight, pureness, alloy and fineness.

An act of 1656 "for the advancing and raising the value of pieces of eight" rated the Mexican pieces of eight and pillar pieces at 4s 8d current money of England. When the act did not have the desired effect, another act was passed on 14 November 1668 for advancing and raising the value of pieces of eight. The preamble stated:

> [I]t hath been found by long Experience that the great want of money is very prejudicial to this Island, in the carrying on the common Trade and Commerce thereof; and that so great a want hath been principally occasioned for that Pieces of Eight have not been fully estimated, but permitted to pass here from Man to Man at too mean Rates; whereupon very much Coyn (coin) hath been exported to Foreign Nations.

The act stated that all pieces of eight, Seville, Mexico and pillar pieces were to pass current in payment between all persons in Barbados "at the rate of Five Shillings per piece current money of England, and that [for] all and every [one of] the half and quarter pieces, and Royals of the said coin, and single Royals of all sorts of Spanish coin in like proportion [previous laws dealing with the values of these coins have been repealed]".[3] As a result of the overrating of the pieces of eight at 5s, exceedingly light pieces of eight were imported. An act concerning Spanish money, passed on 22 December 1669, stated that any person who was in possession of pieces of eight, half and quarter pieces and single ryals which were less in weight or of a baser alloy than was usual would, if convicted, be imprisoned in the common gaol for six months.[4]

PROPOSALS FOR THE ESTABLISHMENT OF A MINT

On account of the scarcity of coins, the governor petitioned the king and the commissioners for foreign plantations between 1661 and 1673 for permission to establish a mint in Barbados. The first proposal in 1661 was to recoin foreign money and bullion to any value that was thought fit.[5] A further proposal was made by the governor in 1669 because there was an inadequate supply of money to support trade, since all things were bought and sold by way of truck or permutation. He suggested that the only way to keep money in the country was by having coin of a lesser valuation than that in England; for example, seven half-crowns in England should be coined into eight half-crowns or 20s for use in Barbados. Subsequent proposals were made suggesting that the mint should coin money that would be current only in Barbados, as per the practice in New England and elsewhere. However, permission was not granted.[6]

QUEEN ANNE'S PROCLAMATION AND THE ACT OF 1707

Towards the beginning of the eighteenth century, the British government considered standardizing the different rates at which the same species of foreign coins were exchanged in the colonies and plantations in America and the inconvenience caused by the indirect practice of attracting money from one plantation to another which was detrimental to trade. It was thought that this practice could only be remedied by reducing all foreign coins to the same current rate. Accordingly the Royal Mint (hereafter the Mint) prepared a table of the weight and intrinsic value of foreign coins in England with a computation for relating these coins to a Seville piece of eight which was to be raised from 4s 6d, its real value, to 6s in the plantations. On the basis of the Mint's report, the royal proclamation of 18 June 1704 was made to settle and ascertain the current rates for foreign coins in Her Majesty's colonies and plantations in America. The rates established were as follows:

	Pennyweight (dwts)	Grains (grs)	Sterling Value Shillings (s)	Pence (d)
Seville pieces of eight, old plate	17	12	4	6
Seville pieces of eight, new plate	14	0	3	7¼
Mexico pieces of eight	17	12	4	6
French ecu of silver Lewis	17	12	4	6
Pillar pieces of eight, old plate	17	12	4	6¾
Peru pieces of eight, old plate	17	12	4	5

(The half, quarter and other parts were rated in proportion to their denominations, and light pieces in proportion to their weight.)

The proclamation also declared that, with effect from 1 January 1705, no Seville, pillar or Mexico pieces of eight, though of the full value of 17½ pennyweight, were to be exchanged above the rate of 6s per piece of current money. All Peru pieces of eight, dollars and other foreign species of silver coins, whether of the same or baser alloy, would be regulated according to their weight and fineness in proportion to the rate established for the pieces of eight of Seville, pillar and Mexico. Thereby, no foreign silver coin of any sort was permitted to exceed the same proportion upon any account whatsoever.[7]

Notwithstanding the imperial proclamation, coins continued to be received at the old rates. The British attorney general advised the Board of Trade that an act of Parliament would be required to make it definitely illegal to receive money at more than its proclamation rate. An act was then passed to this effect in 1707. It stated that after 1 May 1709, any person in the colonies either paying or receiving foreign silver coins above the proclamation rates "should suffer six months' imprisonment without Bail or Main-prize" and also be fined £10 to be divided equally between the Crown and the informer. However, the act stipulated that no one was compelled to receive any of the species of foreign silver coins at the rates mentioned within it or in the proclamation, and further indicated that the queen retained the power to regulate the rates of these coins. Since only silver coins were specified in the act, the West Indian colonies gave independent ratings (by weight) to the gold coins of Spain instead of continuing to treat them as multiples of the silver dollar. The result was that, by stages, the islands passed from a silver to a gold standard of value.

In his book *The Currency of the British Colonies*, published in 1848, James Pennington, a senior Treasury official, stated that the indirect practice of attracting money from one plantation to another probably originated in the false notion that the value of the coins which were made legally current depended not merely on their weight and fineness, but upon the weights or denominations which were assigned to them by law. He was of the opinion that the inconvenience that resulted from this practice was not the artificial and forced removal of money from one colony to another, but the troublesome and complex computations and adjustments which were necessary in the exchange among colonies, and between the colonies and the parent state. Another problem arose from the assignment of disproportionate rates to gold and silver coins.[8]

PAPER BILLS OF CREDIT

The proclamation was observed in Barbados, but several persons exported their money to countries where the proclamation was not adhered to, thereby causing a scarcity of cash in the island. In 1706, Major Dudley Woodbridge introduced a bill to the General Assembly to issue paper money but it was rejected on the third reading. Following the defeat of the bill, Mr William Sharpe (a member of council) and his brother-in-law drafted the Paper Credit Bill. With the support of Alexander Walker in council and John Holder in the assembly, the Paper Credit Act was passed on 18 June 1706 "to supply the want of cash, and to establish a method of credit for persons having real estates in this Island". The act provided, inter alia, for the creation of an office and appointed John Holder as manager. Every person who had an estate of inheritance in Barbados might have a bill of credit signed by Holder to the value of one fourth of the value of the real estate. This bill of credit would pass in Barbados as ready money for the sum mentioned on it. Any person who refused to accept it would pay a penalty of the full value of the bill. The holder of the bill would be charged interest at the rate of 8 per cent per annum, of which Holder would receive 5 per cent. The remainder would be used to pay his staff and cover other expenses.

However, the Paper Credit Act was opposed by the Royal African Company and by British merchants trading with Barbados. On the recommendation of the Commissioners of Trade and Plantations, the act was disallowed by the Privy Council on 21 October 1706, and the queen directed the governor to ensure that the best provision be made for those persons who were obliged to receive such bills as security for debts. As a result of the queen's instructions, an act was passed on 25 April 1707 to ascertain the value of the bills of credit that were issued under the revoked Paper Credit Act. Holder was ordered to refund his commission fee and, in May 1707, he petitioned the council for relief from refunding the sum of £2,592 6s 10d. The council agreed that he should not be made to refund the money, but the assembly disagreed. Holder then appealed to the Commissioners of Trade and Plantations, but that body also ruled that his commission should be refunded. A Committee of the General Assembly appointed "to examine who were the promoters and advisers of the Act" presented its report on 5 June 1707. It documented the origin of the scheme; the members of council and others who supported the act; the amounts of money received for their support; as well as the attempted bribery of Major Woodbridge by Holder.

Between 1708 and 1716, several acts were passed to rectify problems created by the Paper Bill Act. The proliferation of the paper bills in some of the American colonies caused an order in council to be made in 1720. Governors of all plantations in America were instructed that, in future, they should not pass a law allowing bills of credit to be issued in lieu of money for payment to the governor, the council, the assembly, or to any other person without inserting a clause that such acts should not come into force until they had been approved and confirmed by the monarch. An exception, however, would be made for laws that sought to raise a public revenue to defray the government's debts according to the instructions given to the respective governors.[9] The public debt in 1722 amounted to between £20,000 and £30,000; in order to extinguish the debt, an act was passed "to raise a levy and to establish a method to supply the want of cash for the payment of the public debts". The treasurer was directed to prepare bills of credit not exceeding £24,000 with interest at the rate of 6 per cent per annum to be paid off in six years. Merchants in London who traded with Barbados objected to the act, leading to its revocation on 22 August 1724.[10]

British merchants in 1735 petitioned the Board of Trade regarding the disparity in the rates assigned to the silver and gold coins in the colonies. As a consequence of the complaints, the House of Commons sent two addresses to the king, in June 1739, requesting information from the colonies and plantations about the amount of paper bills or bills of credit issued in 1700 and after, and the provisions made for discharging them; the rates at which gold and silver had been purchased and sold for the years 1700, 1710, 1720, 1730.[11] The following reply from Mr Dottin, president of the council, to the Commissioners of Trade and Plantations on 9 November 1739 gave a comprehensive review of the state of currency in Barbados from 1700 to 1739:

> I have diligently inquired and find that no paper credit was established in this island in 1700 nor at any time before or since but in 1705 when paper bills of credit to the value of £7,000 were issued for the payment of a tax then laid on the inhabitants, and in 1706 when an Act "to supply the want of cash and to establish a method of credit for persons having real estates in this island" passed here 18 June 1706, empowering the treasurer to issue bills of credit by way of loans for one year to any person who should apply for the same to the value of one fourth of their estates, which bills were then directed to pass as current cash and be received and allowed in payments accordingly, in consequence whereof large sums were issued. But the bills being of little or no credit and occasioning all the gold and silver to be sent off the island and greatly discouraging the trade thereof, Queen Anne by order in council dated 21 October 1706 declared her disallowance of the said Act and signified her royal will and pleasure to this government that all possible care should be taken and the best provision made that could be that such who had been obliged to receive such bills, and the persons to whom

any debts were owing and had been obliged to part with legal securities for such bills, should be no sufferers thereby but be restored as far as might be by some new law to the same state they were in before the passing [of] the said Act; and to prevent a law of the like or of any extraordinary nature till the sovereign's pleasure is first known therein, which has occasioned no other paper currency since to be established in this island.

In 1700 and till 1 January, 1704 (i.e. 1705 new style) foreign silver coin passed in this island by tale so that generally light money only was paid and received here. For if what was offered would by a standard be of greater or less value than it was offered at, it was taken according to its denomination of whole, quarter and eighth pieces, whereby a great deal of the foreign coins passing here were clipped and made very light, and there was then no complaint made of the want of cash in this island. The gold that was then current were pistoles which passed at 20s and guineas at 25s. There was then seldom any uncoined gold sold in this island, and the little silver that was sold was purchased at 5s per ounce. Queen Anne by proclamation dated 18 June 1704, published in this island 24 August following and [which] was to take place and be enforced [as of] 1 January . . . , having settled and ascertained the current rates of foreign coins in HM's colonies and plantations in America, all the light money that had been before current was before that settlement took place paid away in discharge of debts then owing in the island; and the cash having then centred in the hands of merchants and other traders, who having advices that the neighbouring colonies and plantations had not paid that strict observance to HM's proclamation as had been done in this island, most or all of the cash was soon afterwards sent off from hence, which occasioned the prejudicial Act beforementioned to be passed in this island for supplying the want thereof. And from the said 1 January, 1704/5 till this time all silver coins are accounted received, taken and paid according to the ratio and standard directed by the said proclamation. And when moidores were first introduced into this island, without any regard to their weight, they passed currently at 35s each as well as pistoles at 20s and guineas at 22s until 1715 or 1716 when the principal merchants agreeing to take pistoles at 22s 6d, guineas at 27s 6d and moidores at 37s 6d, they have ever since till this time passed at those rates; and not many years since many pieces of new coined Spanish gold have been introduced and pass current, the whole piece at £5 and the other pieces in proportion thereto. We have lately a very bad silver mostly current among us of a very base alloy of a Spanish coin called or distinguished by the name of pistereens which pass by weight; but a French coin made for the payment of their soldiers abroad are reckoned much better silver, yet they pass currently by tale at 7½d but weigh generally about 7d and under and are much esteemed by the inhabitants but few remain long in the island, being carried to HM's Leeward Islands and other places where the standard and weighing of money being little regarded, this island is very often drained of all its cash. Uncoined gold is generally sold here at £4 10s per ounce and silver at 5s 6d per ounce, and the exchange betwixt this island and Great Britain for many years past has been 28 to 32 per cent but most commonly at 30.[12]

After replies were received from other colonies, governors were instructed not to assent to acts for issuing bills of credit without a clause suspending their execution until the Crown's pleasure was known.[13] Available records indicate that between 1731 and 1790 no local acts were passed relating to currency; however, local proclamations as well as imperial acts and proclamations were passed relating to paper money and currency in the colonies. In spite of the instructions to the governors, the issue of paper money continued in the colonies and on the plantations in America. An imperial act was therefore passed in 1750 for restraining the issue of paper bills of credit in the New England colonies. In 1764, British merchants trading with the colonies in America complained to the Board of Trade regarding the legal tender of the paper bills on the grounds that it was in violation of the imperial legislation. An imperial act was passed in 1764 "to prevent paper bills of credit to be issued in any of H.M.'s Colonies or Plantations in America from being declared legal tender in payments of money, and to prevent the legal tender of such bills as are now subsisting from being prolonged beyond the periods for calling in and sinking the same". However, on account of the scarcity of gold and silver coins in several of the colonies and on the plantations in America, an imperial act was passed in 1773 which provided that, after 1 September 1773, paper bills could be issued by the treasurers as legal tender and received by them for the payment of duties or taxes.

DEBASED AND MUTILATED COINS

Mr Dottin, in his report (already mentioned), outlined the state of the debased coins in Barbados up to 1739. By about 1770, counterfeit coins, including British copper and foreign coins exported from England, began to circulate in the West Indies. American traders accepted only genuine coins and local trade was increasingly carried on by lightweight pieces. On 20 October 1789, the council discussed the practice of debasing the current coin by cutting and clipping and other illegal means, and a proclamation was subsequently issued by President Frere on 27 October 1789 directing all justices of the peace "strictly to attend to all complaints thereof, and diligently to put the laws in force against all such offenders, and hereby to exhort all persons to endeavour to discover those who are guilty of such shameful offences, that they may be brought to proper punishment for their fraudulent practices".[14] A committee of the assembly appointed to advise on a policy for dealing with this issue recommended, on 18 May 1790, the penalties to be included in an act, but proposed that the act should not take effect until the king had approved it.[15]

Notwithstanding the imperial act of 1707 and the local proclamation of 1789, the practice of the debasing of coins continued, therefore a proclamation was issued on 24 March 1791 which required justices of the peace to investigate complaints about violations of the imperial act.[16] In view of the scarcity of legal silver coin, and to clarify the position of cut money in circulation, a second proclamation was issued on 28 March 1791 "to prevent any misconception in the minds of people concerning the silver coin . . . and to obviate as much as may be proper all difficulties in the way of trade and barter within this Island". It also stated that "although the base silver coin lately current and in circulation, cannot legally be passed as heretofore; yet the same is never the less allowable to pass by weight, according to the proper and legal standard by weight and not otherwise".[17]

The mutilation was not confined to silver coins but was also inflicted upon gold coins. In order to address the deficiency in the act of Queen Anne with respect to the gold coin, an act was passed on 8 June 1791 "Against the forging and debasing of Foreign Gold Coins, and such Foreign Gold Coins as are now, or shall hereafter be made current and taken and received by General Consent in Payment in this Island; and against clipping, diminishing, and impairing of the same; and for preventing the bringing into this Island any counterfeit Foreign Gold Coins". Persons convicted of clipping, counterfeiting, or filing the current gold coin would be sentenced to death; and the importers of all diminished or debased coin, besides forfeiting the imported coin, were liable to a penalty of £500. The act was published by the beat of drum at Bridge Town, Hole Town, Speights Town and Oistins Town.[18]

A joint committee of the assembly and the council reported that the act was only to stop the mutilation of the specie and that consideration should be given to standardizing the value of the gold coin according to its weight or otherwise.[19] Another joint committee appointed in June 1791 recommended that foreign gold should not pass by tale but by weight and that the standard weights of those species of gold coin current in Barbados should be as follows:

	Weighing at least		Currency Value		
	Pennyweight	Grains	Pounds	Shillings	Pence
	(dwts)	(grs)	(£)	(s)	(d)
Joe	16	16	5	0	0
Moidore	6	5	1	17	6
Double doubloon	15	14	4	10	0
Rider	5	22	1	15	0
Louis d'or	5	22	1	13	9
French and Portugal guineas	4	16	1	7	6
English guineas	5	8	1	10	0

(2¾d should be allowed for every grain short of the above standard weights, and a clause should be inserted in the bill prohibiting the importation of Joes of the value of 50s below the weight of 9 dwts. The penalty for anyone doing so is that they would forfeit the imported coin and be fined £500 and the smaller kinds of the same coinage in the same proportion.)[20]

The assembly did not accept all of the recommendations, particularly those relating to the weights of some coins and, during the next several weeks, bills passed, either by the assembly or council, were rejected. During that period, the assembly received a petition from merchants and others objecting to a bill under consideration and they proposed "that to settle all the perfect coins at a general rate, as nearly approaching to their former value as possible, and to make the diminished coins pass by weight at 2¾d the real value of the grain of gold in this market, is the most safe, proper, honourable, and effectual mode of remedying the present inconveniences and restoring a currency which shall be lasting and permanent".[21] When the council and assembly could not agree on an acceptable bill, Governor Parry issued a proclamation on 4 August 1791 "in order to resort at once to the true and only equitable principle of fixing all foreign coins at a standard proportionate to the legal coin of Great Britain and of keeping the different species of foreign gold coins aforesaid as nearly as may be to their known weight and standard". He directed that after the publication of the proclamation, the foreign gold coins should pass and be current in Barbados at the following rates:

	Weight		Currency Value		
	Pennyweights	Grains	Pounds	Shillings	Pence
	dwts	grs	(£)	(s)	(d)
Portugal johannes	18	10	5	0	0
Portugal half johannes	9	5	2	10	0
Portugal moidore	6	21	1	17	6
Spanish doubloon	17	8	4	10	0
Spanish half doubloon	8	16	2	5	0

(The sum of 2d 3 farthings current money was to be allowed for every grain of gold found to be deficient.)[22]

An act was passed on 16 November 1791 "for indemnifying the Treasurer and Storekeeper from the loss arising to the public from the cut and mutilated coins, received by them for the public levies and debts, previous to his Excellency's Proclamation respecting the said coin".[23]

Governors were informed in May 1798 that a bill would be presented to Parliament to prevent the export of base copper coins from the United Kingdom to the West Indies and that they should issue a proclamation recommending all persons to weigh the gold and silver coins then current, and to state in the proclamation what weight the respective coins should be, making allowances for reasonable wear. The copper coins in circulation consisted entirely of farthings and were largely used by slaves.[24] An imperial act was passed on 21 June 1798 "to prevent the exportation of base coin to His Majesty's Colonies in the West Indies and America". The preamble stated that

> various base copper coins made to the resemblance and similitude of the foreign copper coins called Tempes and Sous Marques have been exported from this Kingdom to the Island of Martinique in the West Indies under the denomination of wrought copper; and . . . base coins made to the similitude and resemblance of

the foreign gold and silver coins called Johannes and Dollars have been circulated in His Majesty's Colonies in the West Indies and in other His Majesty's Colonies in America.

The act decreed that any persons exporting these base coins to Martinique or the colonies would forfeit them and be fined £200 and double the value of such coin for every offence.[25] Martinique raised its ratings and some other West Indian islands followed suit in order to prevent their coin from being exported. The secretary of state issued a second circular in December, pointing out that the previous circular had been misunderstood and that no alteration either in the nominal value of the coins or in the relative values of the metals ought at any time to be made without his consent.[26]

As the weighing of the clipped and other silver money became inconvenient, especially to the lower and poorer classes who were unable to dispose of the coins without great difficulty and loss, a local act was passed on 19 March 1799 "To prevent the further currency of the clipt, and other Silver Money by weight, and for calling in the same, and for indemnifying the Treasurer from the Loss arising to the Public from the Deficiency of such clipped and other Silver Coin as hath been or shall be passed into the receipt of the Treasury". With effect from 5 April, no clipped or other silver money by weight was legal tender. Persons who owed levies and assessments could pay such silver coins into the Treasury at the weighted value up to 5 July 1799. Persons who owed no taxes were required to take these coins to the Treasury before 5 April. The treasurer was directed to select "such good round pieces of dollars, crown pieces, half dollars, quarter dollars, two bit pieces, bits and half bits, as well as all such clipt monies as may be by him deemed necessary for a currency to pass by tale as change" and dispose of them according to his discretion. This transaction was met by paying treasury bills of 8 months' date for the old silver.[27] After the passing of this act, it was reported that the silver money was as good as could be wished, except for the half bit, formed by cutting the bits into halves, but which were frequently thirds. The half bits were convenient for use by the lower classes and passed in small payments for 15 farthings.[28]

2

The Introduction of British Coins

BEFORE THE PASSING of the Emancipation Act, it was generally the merchants, artisans and freedmen who used coins of lower denomination. The planters' main requirements were for estate supplies and food and clothing for their slaves. They obtained finance for these commodities largely from Great Britain, where the British merchants, who served as their factors, would advance supplies and make other payments prior to the sale of the sugar crop. Local merchants and moneylenders also provided credit and loans. The colonists obtained foreign coins, especially the doubloon and the Spanish dollar, from traders, but the American traders usually demanded cash for their cargoes rather than local produce, which they could obtain from the French islands at a lower price.

The mutilation of the coins in the West Indies continued into the nineteenth century and, in May 1812, Governor Beckwith wrote to Secretary Bathurst of the serious problems that would arise from the lack of specie in the West Indies, especially in Barbados, because of the recent debasement of the coins in other islands and the demand for those of a superior value. He suggested that £40,000 in dollars or doubloons should be sent to the commissariat in Barbados.[1] Lord Bathurst did not believe that this amount could be remitted without prejudice to Britain's other commitments and, in turn, suggested to the Committee of the Privy Council for Trade (hereafter referred to as the Committee for Trade) that, in the first instance, £30,000 in copper coins should be provided. At that time, the Mint was not coining copper coins.[2] The situation was further exacerbated by the action of some governments which passed acts or issued proclamations that sought to remedy the increasing depreciation and fluctuation in the weight or value of the coins.[3]

In 1815, the Committee for Trade reviewed the state of the coins in the West Indies, in particular those of the lower denominations, and proposed that special coins should be issued for use in the colonies. Mr G.W. Jordan, the Barbados agent in England, in reply to a questionnaire from the Committee for Trade to the island's agents, indicated the main coins that were current in Barbados and their value:

	Currency Value	
	Shillings	Pence
	(s)	(d)
Dollar	6	3 or 10 bits
Half dollar	3	1½ or 5 bits
Quarter dollar	1	6¾ or 2½ bits
Pistereens	1	3 or 2 bits
Pistereen bits		7½
Crimbal or Isle du Vent bits		7½

There were also dollar half bits, Crimbal half bits, pistereens and cut half bits valued at 3¾d currency. The Isle du Vent bits were French coins that France made for their Windward Islands colonies, and which Mr Jordan understood were called Crimbal after the person who first introduced them into circulation in Barbados. The copper coins consisted principally of farthings.[4] In Barbados, as noted above, the dollar was rated at 6s 3d currency. However, the doubloon was rated at 90s. At this rate, the doubloon was undervalued and the gold coins began to disappear from circulation. In order to stop the loss of gold coins, the merchants held a public meeting in 1817 at which it was agreed that the value of the doubloon should be raised to 100s currency or $16 instead of 96s currency, which was at that time the bullion trade rating for gold.[5] This, however, now resulted in the doubloon being overvalued; thus, while Barbados attracted gold coins, silver dollars and small change were driven from the island.

Following a visit by the inspector of hospitals to the Leeward and Windward islands in 1817, the secretary of war recommended that the soldiers be paid daily instead of monthly to induce them to apply some part of their pay to the purchase of fruit and vegetables rather than on rum. The Treasury issued instructions to send £4,000 in British copper coins to the commissariats in the West Indies for this purpose. In order to encourage the inhabitants of the islands to accept these coins during business transactions, the commissariats were instructed to receive them either in exchange for bills drawn on the Treasury or in exchange for dollars at the rate of 56 penny pieces for the Spanish dollar, which was then issued to the soldiers at the rate of 4s 8d. Governors were directed to implement measures that would ensure the use of copper coins.[6] In response, Governor Combermere issued a proclamation on 3 March 1819,[7] which directed that from 24 March 1819, copper coins should be exchanged at the following rates:

> 56 penny pieces or 112 half penny pieces for a Spanish dollar
>
> 28 penny pieces or 56 half penny pieces for a half dollar
>
> 14 penny pieces or 28 half penny pieces for a quarter dollar
>
> 10 penny pieces or 20 half penny pieces for a pistereen
>
> 5 penny pieces or 10 half penny pieces for a bit
>
> 1 penny sterling for penny halfpenny currency
>
> Half penny sterling for 3 farthings currency

The copper coins were not well accepted throughout the West Indies, especially in Jamaica where the blacks and even beggars refused to accept them.

ANCHOR MONEY

The proposal for special coins was raised again by Lord Bathurst in September 1819 because of the debased state of the silver coins in the West Indies. The island agents were informed that the Mint would coin silver coins for the colonies, consisting of quarters, eighths and sixteenths of a dollar of the same standard as the Spanish dollar. The Mint would retain the usual seignorage for coinage.[8] Governors were subsequently told that the Treasury would send these coins, from which no seignorage had been taken, to the commissariat in the West Indies for payment to the troops. It was hoped that, by their gradual introduction, the West Indies would be provided with a currency of the same standard and denomination. However, if the colonies wanted an additional supply, they would be required to pay the commissariat in the colony dollars to an equivalent amount.[9] These coins were referred to as "anchor money" because they had anchor inscription on one side (with an impression of the king's army on the obverse). Governor Warde issued a proclamation on 5 February 1823 which stated that the coins would be legal tender in Barbados as of 25 February.[10] These coins were first sent to Mauritius in 1820, but only two remittances amounting to $178,070 were sent to the West Indies in June and July 1822.[11]

At some of its branches in the West Indies, the Colonial Bank in 1852 held about £20,000 in worn and defaced silver coins consisting of £10,700 in anchor money (£5,250 in Barbados), £8,000 in foreign coins and the remainder in British coins. The bank tried to make a deal with the Treasury that it would return the coins, at its own expense, to England where they would ask the Mint to recoin them, free of charge, into shillings. The bank would then ship these shillings back to the West Indies at its own expense.[12] The proposal was not accepted because there was no seignorage on the anchor money and therefore these coins could not be accepted by tale. Also, the law did not permit free coinage. With respect to the British coins, however, if they were found unfit for circulation, they could be sent to the Mint for recoinage.[13]

PROCLAMATION OF 1825

In 1825, the British government decided to introduce British silver coins as the circulating medium in all of its colonies. There were two main reasons for this change in policy. The British act of 1816 had established gold as the sole standard of value and had relegated the new silver coins to tokens; however, by the end of 1816, the recently constructed Mint was in full working condition and able to provide more coins than were required for internal circulation. The second reason for the introduction of silver coins was the closure in 1820 of the Spanish mints in South America when the new republics became independent and the supply of Spanish silver coins to the West Indies ceased. An order in council, issued on 23 March 1825, stated that

> in all those Colonies where the Spanish dollar is now, either by law, fact or practice, considered as a legal tender for the discharge of debts, or where the duties to Government are rated or collected, or the individuals have a right to pay in that description of coin, . . . a tender and payment of British silver money to the amount of 4s 4d should be considered as equivalent to the tender or payment of one Spanish dollar, and so in proportion for any greater or less amount of debt.

Holders of British silver coins could demand from the commissariat, bills on the Treasury at thirty days' sight (that is, payment was due in thirty days) by paying £103 in British silver for a bill of £100. British copper coins were made legal tender up to 12d for one payment.[14] £50,000 in British silver coins and £200 in copper coins were shipped to the Windward and Leeward Islands command.[15] Prior to the issue of the proclamation, the Treasury transmitted detailed instructions to the commissariats with respect to the exchange for bills upon the Treasury, pay and allowances to the troops and payment to contractors.[16] The commissariat in Barbados, which was the headquarters for the army in the Leeward and Windward Islands, Tobago, Trinidad, and British Guiana, previously received its money in Spanish, Mexican and Columbian coins, rather than British coins, from the British Treasury or from the commissariat in Jamaica, which they would use to pay the troops and local contractors.[17] Prior to the advent of commercial banks, the commissariat was where bills of exchange were obtained.

The local proclamation, dated 6 September 1825,[18] included, for the convenience of the public, the following comparative scale of the exact sterling value of the money and coins then circulating in Barbados:

Coins	Barbados		Currency Bits	British Sterling		
	Pounds	Shillings	Pence	Shillings	Pence	
	(£)	(s)	(d)	(s)	(d)	
Half-crown	3	7¼ ⅓	5¹⁹⁄₃	2	6	British coin
Shilling	1	5¼ ¾	2⅔	1	0	British coin
Sixpence		8½ ⅔	1⅔		6	British coin

Coins	Barbados Currency			Bits	British Sterling		
	Pounds (£)	Shillings (s)	Pence (d)		Shillings (s)	Pence (d)	
Dollar	6	3	10		4	4	Foreign
Half dollar	3	1½	5		2	2	coins to
Quarter dollar	1	6¾	2½		1	1	which a
Eighth of a dollar		9	1¼			6½	British or
Sixteenth of a dollar		4¹¹⁄₁₆				3¼	sterling
Spanish peceta or pestareen			2			10	value was
Bit piece or ½ franc of 10 sols						5	affixed

In the opinion of the deputy commissary general (hereafter referred to as DCG), the coins issued from the military chest were limited because the Barbados government did not sufficiently promote their circulation. He further noted that the fractions of the money inhibited their circulation except at a small loss.[19] The DCG experienced great difficulty in keeping the one penny copper coins in circulation and suspected that many of them were being exported. He therefore requested that only half pence and farthings, especially farthings, be sent by the Treasury because they would be more useful for small purchases and would better correspond to the needs of local demand.[20] In January 1827, the Treasury complained to the commissariat that

> when British money is issued from the military chests to the paymasters or others, it is exchanged for dollars, or other circulating medium, and the silver money is returned into the chest for bills on this Board, instead of being paid to the men, by which measure only it would get into circulation, and supersede the circulation of dollars and other foreign coins, for which it is, in Their Lordships' opinion in all respects better adapted.[21]

The Treasury believed that the money could be returned from many stations to England at a charge less than 3 per cent. With effect from the twenty-fourth of the month after the publication of a notice, the rate of exchange for British silver was reduced in 1827 from £103 to £101 10s for a bill of £100.[22] The rating of Spanish coins for concurrent circulation with British coins resulted in a substantial loss in pay to the soldier and, in order to ameliorate the loss, the army rate for the doubloon was reduced in 1835 from 69s 4d to 66s. The basis for the reduction was stated in the following extract from the minutes of the Treasury Board:

> In fixing an army rate on foreign gold coins, My Lords consider it to be a desirable object to render it, if possible, indifferent to the soldier whether he receives his pay in those coins, or in foreign silver money; and as the doubloon is intrinsically equivalent to about 15 5/21 dollars, and, in paying the army on foreign stations, the dollar is valued at 4s. 4d., the corresponding value of the gold piece may, with sufficient accuracy, be considered to be 66s. Accordingly, Their Lordships are pleased to direct, that so long as it shall be considered expedient to continue the army rate fixed on the Spanish dollar in the year 1825, the doubloon shall be issued to the troops at the rate of sixty six shillings, and the several divisions of that coin at proportional rates.[23]

In his book *Four Years' Residence in the West Indies, 1826–1829*, F.N. Bayley wrote:

> In Barbados the current coins are Doubloons, Joes, Dollars, Half Dollars, Quarter Dollars, a silver piece called a "Bitt and Twopence", a Fivepenny Pence, and a Halfpence. 10 Bitts make one dollar. A bitt is 7½d. currency, and a dollar is 6s. 3d.

Coins	Currency			Army Sterling		
	(£)	(s)	(d)	(£)	(s)	(d)
Doubloon	5	0	0	3	9	4
Joe	2	10	0	1	14	8
Dollar		6	3		4	4
1 Bitt & 2d.		9¼	6½			
Bitt		7¼	5			
Fivepenny		4¾	3¼			
½ Bitt		3¾	2½			

[Rule to reduce British Sterling into Currency: Multiply the amount sterling by 75 and divide the result by 52. To reduce any amount sterling into dollars, bring the amount sterling into pence, and divide by 52, the quotient will be the number of dollars required.][24]

Following the independence of the South American states, the Spanish mints in those states were closed and the supply of pillared dollars to the West Indies ceased. However, the new states established their own mints and issued dollars which were called "new dollars". However, they were not as well known as the old Spanish pillared dollar, and so they bore a premium of 20 per cent. When the British Parliament made a grant to Barbados to relieve the sufferers of the ravages of the 1831 hurricane, a part ($123,847) of the money was sent in the new dollars. Their extensive circulation in the West Indies removed some of the prejudice against them, but the Spanish dollar still bore a premium of 1 per cent to 2½ per cent, although merchants and other well-informed persons were aware that they were of the same weight and fineness as the Spanish dollar. The DCG suggested that an assay should be made to remove any prejudice which remained in the minds of the ignorant and uninformed part of the West Indian community.[25]

On account of the embarrassment caused by the difficulty in making suitable remittances to the colonies, the Treasury asked the Mint to make an assay of the new dollars, including their fractional parts, as well as the gold doubloons and their divisions which were current in the West Indies.[26] The assay revealed that the new dollars were as valuable as, or rather better in weight and fineness than, the Spanish dollars previously coined in Mexico.[27] Governors were advised that if difficulties were experienced in the free circulation of the new dollars, they were to issue an announcement and proclamation that the coins should be received and issued by the government's agencies and authorities at the same rate as the old pillar dollars.[28] Since there were no problems with their circulation in Barbados, it was only necessary to publish a notice to this effect.[29]

When the need for coins of the lower denominations became urgent, a bill was introduced in the House of Assembly in June 1834 "to make the English gold coins called sovereigns a legal tender in the payment of debts at a value of 30 shillings Currency". The House of Assembly appointed a committee "to take into consideration the propriety of introducing the coins of Great Britain into circulation in this Island at a fair Island currency valuation".[30] The committee believed that the introduction of British coins would prevent the constant fluctuations in exchange caused by the scarcity of doubloons. Doubloons were scarcely used because it was difficult to obtain either small gold coins or silver coins in exchange for them. The committee recalled that British coins did not remain in circulation because the local proclamation issued in 1825 took the Spanish dollar as the standard and valued the half-crown at 3s 7¼d $^{1}/_{13}$. Since the doubloon was passing in Barbados for £5 currency, 27 half-crowns could have been purchased for £3 7s 6d sterling, but a doubloon in England could be purchased for £3 4s, therefore a profit of 3s 6d sterling could be made on each doubloon. The committee believed that reducing the value of the doubloon would interfere with all contracts which had taken place during that period, and would increase the difficulties of debtors, and would be an act of gross injustice. They were of the opinion that the value of the doubloon at £5 currency should be taken as the standard, so they fixed a currency value on the British coins. The committee found, on inquiry, that the average price of a doubloon in London was about £3 4s sterling and, as its rate in Barbados was £5 currency, proposed that the value of the sovereign should be £1 11s 3d currency and the value of other British silver coins should be in proportion to the sovereign. The committee recommended the following currency values for British coins:

	Currency		
	Pounds (£)	Shillings (s)	Pence (d)
Sovereign	1	11	3
Half-sovereign		15	7½
Crown		7	9¾
Half-crown		3	10¾ ¼
Shilling		1	6¾
Sixpence			9¼ ²⁄₄

The committee also suggested that the introduction of colonial copper coins, relative to the currency value placed on the British silver coin, would be of the greatest benefit to the island. The coins suggested were pence, half pence, farthings and the fourths of farthings. It was expected that they would contribute to the functioning of the apprenticeship system, that was about to be implemented, and would be beneficial during the time of freedom which would follow the period of apprenticeship.[31]

Following the report by the committee, in July 1834 the House of Assembly passed a bill which made £156 5s currency equivalent to £100 sterling as opposed to the legal value of £144 4s 7d 5/13 currency.[32] Some merchants, who claimed that the legislature was dominated by the landed interest, objected to the change in the value of the currency. When the governor sent the merchants' petition to the secretary of state, he stated that the bill was an attempt to enable debtors to pay off debts with less real money than they were contracted at and to save the export merchants, who had nearly all the planters in their power, at the expense of importers who required fair bills of exchange for their goods. In his opinion, the bill would change the value of the dollar from 4s 4d to 4s and cost the public about £10,000 a year. He concluded that "the design is weak, selfish and unprincipled, and if such a Bill should come before me I would not entertain it for five minutes".[33]

MINT REGULATIONS

A proclamation of 13 April 1831 made the following coins current and lawful money in England:

Gold   –   Double sovereign, sovereign and half-sovereign

Silver –   Crown, half-crown, shilling and sixpence

Copper –   Penny, halfpenny and farthing

In the early years of the 1830s, there was an increasing demand for silver coins in England and for small silver coins to pay the labourers and apprentices in the West Indies. In 1835, Mr Colquhoun, an agent in England for the planters in some of the West Indian islands, asked the secretary of state to direct the Mint to supply the planters in the colonies with small silver coins.[34] The Mint suggested that the coins should be restricted to the 3d, coined only for the use of His Majesty's Maundy, and the 1½d coined especially for Jamaica, because no copper coin would circulate in that island. The Mint stated that since the 3d and 1½d coins were not made current by proclamation, they could only be received at the Mint according to their intrinsic value. It recommended that £5,000 of these coins should be minted for the other West Indian colonies in such proportions as might be required.[35] The committee of West Indian merchants and planters in England was informed that it was not the government's intention to send these coins to the colonies at the public expense, unless they were required for use by the military.[36] The DCG of Barbados was also informed that these coins should not be received in payment for Treasury bills at the fixed rate of 1½ per cent, as were the coins which were made current by proclamation.[37]

Prior to the issue of the regulations, all applications to purchase coins from the Mint had to be submitted to the Treasury. If the applications were approved, directions would then be given to the Mint or the Bank of England to supply the amount required. If the Mint did not have the coins in stock, the applicant would have to make an advance to the Mint to enable it to purchase the bullion to effect the coinage. In the case of the commissariats, the Treasury would notify the Mint of the value and denominations of the coins to be remitted and then reimburse the Mint for the coins supplied or the bullion required. When South American dollars were required, the Bank of England would purchase them for the Treasury. An official in the Treasury would then be responsible for the shipment of all coins to the commissariats. As a result of several applications for these coins, in October 1835 the Treasury authorized the Mint to issue regulations which stated that no person could receive the coins without an order from the Treasury; that the 3d and 1½d coins would be made up in bags of £25 value, and the half-crowns, shillings and sixpences in bags of £100; and that no fractional parts of a bag of any denomination would be delivered.[38] The original intent of the regulations was to prevent a superabundance of the currency, especially the sixpence and upwards, and to increase the recent coinage of small coins. A new silver 4d was issued in February 1836 and a similar regulation was published for this coin.[39]

A proclamation issued in July 1838 for a new coinage of gold, silver and copper from the £5 to the farthing ordered that, in addition to the other monies, the "Queen's Maundy shall pass and be received, as current and lawful money of the United Kingdom of Great Britain and Ireland, at the value of 4d, 3d, 2d and 1d, as the case may be". The Mint, in November 1838, was authorized to issue the 2d and 4d coins which were more convenient fractions of some of the larger coins circulating in the West Indies than the 1½d coin.[40] The Treasury in 1841 suspended its restriction on the delivery from the Mint of any other silver coin than the 3d or 4d pieces. The Mint was, therefore, at liberty to coin such moderate amounts of shillings, sixpences and any other denomination of silver coinage as might be required to meet demands authorized by the Treasury.[41] The 3d was made current in the United Kingdom in 1845 following representation to the Mint that the coin afforded additional convenience for the purpose of change; its issue was subjected to the same regulation as the 4d.[42] However, in the following year, the Treasury, for the convenience of the public, agreed that its approval would not be required for the issue of the 4d and 3d pieces but stated that it would review this decision annually.[43]

SCARCITY OF COINS

In 1836, small denominations of silver coins became scarce, largely because of inappropriate rates of exchange but also because of the inconvenient fractional parts fixed by the 1825 proclamation and the high price of the gold coins. The situation became so acute that the House of Assembly passed a bill "to fix an Island currency value on British silver coins and to make the same legal tender to a certain amount".[44] The bill proposed that the English shilling should pass for a quarter dollar, or 1s 6¾d Barbados currency. Forty-six persons signed a petition asking the governor not to sign the bill without giving them the opportunity to show that the measure was injurious to a large section of the mercantile interests, particularly retailers, because the local proclamation of 1825 rated £100 sterling for £144 4s 7$\frac{5}{13}$ d. currency while the bill increased the value to £156 5s currency. They recommended that the dollar be adopted as the money of account because that coin was best suited to the habits and necessaries of the people and also because all contracts were entered into with reference to the dollar. The bill was subsequently vetoed by the governor on the advice of the attorney general.[45]

When the petition was sent to the secretary of state, the governor referred to the problem of the scarcity of small coins to pay the apprenticed labourers for their extra time and for working on their free day (on Saturday) during the crop season. The labourers worked only for cash and never credit, such was their distrust of white men. He was concerned about the fluctuation of sterling as well as the balance of trade with America being against the colonies, because the American traders would take only money in exchange for their commodities. The governor suggested that, if £10,000 or £20,000 in anchor money were remitted for the expenditure of the army, it would be of great temporary relief. Although previous issues of these coins had been exported mainly to British Guiana, he believed that the speculation had ceased.[46] In order to supply the commissariats with coins, the Treasury made arrangements with agents in

Mexico to send coins to the DCG of Jamaica, who would remit them to the other DCGs in the region. On some occasions, the supply would be inadequate and the DCG of Barbados and Jamaica would be compelled to request remittances from the Treasury. As a result of these applications, the chancellor of the exchequer informed the Treasury that the Bank of England had 20,000 guineas (£21,000) which they had sent to Barbados. There was no demand in Barbados, mainly because the guinea was no longer current, or in Grenada, where a few had been sent on an experimental basis.[47] The coins were subsequently returned to England where the Mint recoined them into sovereigns.

During the reaping of the crop in 1836, the scarcity of small coins became serious. Since the governor had not received a reply to his proposal for a supply of anchor money, the Privy Council, in order to assist the planters, agreed to issue a proclamation fixing the currency value for sterling coins for six months to take effect from 13 April 1836:

Sterling	Current Money	
	Shillings	Pence
	(s)	(d)
Shilling	1	6
Sixpence		9
Fourpenny piece, called a groat		6
Threepence		4½

The effect of the proclamation was that the dollar was made equal to 4s 2d sterling. The measure had the desired effect because the Barbados treasurer bought only £500 sterling worth of small British silver coins from the commissariat in exchange for doubloons and dollars. The governor again requested that a supply of anchor money be paid to the troops, thereby enabling it to get into rapid circulation and possibly prevent the recurrence of a deficiency.[48] The Treasury did not approve the coinage of anchor money at the expense of the British public because British silver coins had recently been remitted to the commissariat as well as to individual merchants in the West Indies.[49]

In the meantime, in some of the islands, the nominal value of British coins had been raised to such an extent that the dollar was driven out of circulation for internal commerce. British silver was also exported and not returned to the military chest for the purchase of treasury bills. Since the DCG was unable to supply these coins, he requested a remittance of £15,000 in British silver coins from the Treasury for his command.[50] Some colonial legislatures, without permission from the secretary of state, adopted measures for revising and altering the rates of local monies of account. Governors were instructed by the secretary of state not to permit any act, ordinance, proclamation or regulation to come into operation relating to the local currency and circulating medium or to the rates at which coins should pass current or be legal tender unless he had given them his prior consent, because these measures affected transactions, particularly those with the commissariat.[51]

When the proclamation issued in April was due to expire, a second proclamation[52] was issued on 30 September 1836 for six months to take effect from 13 October. In addition to the coins mentioned in the previous proclamation, this one included the silver crown (five-shilling piece), which was to pass at 7s 6d current money, and the silver half-crown (2s 6d), which was to pass at 3s 9d. However, at the expiration of the proclamation, the shortage of small coins recurred. The new governor, Sir Evan MacGregor, concluded that the recent instruction precluded him from renewing the proclamation. At a public meeting, held on 2 May 1837, it was noted that the the shortage of small denominations of silver coins would harm the planters and apprenticed labourers, especially the latter, who were prevented from obtaining employment during their extra hours and other free days. In the opinion of those at the meeting, the best means of placing the circulating medium on a wholesome and permanent footing would be "by preserving the old and accustomed metallic currency based on the Spanish Dollar". They suggested that this could be accomplished by the Mint coining fractional parts of the dollar to be used as legal tender in the colonies, not only by the commissariat, but also by all persons who desired to purchase them. Those at the meeting called on the public to receive the British silver coins at the rates specified in the expired proclamation. A resolution proposed at the meeting to limit the tender of British silver coins to 40s was defeated.[53] When the resolutions were submitted to the secretary of state, the Treasury agreed to the renewal of the proclamation, but with respect to the supply of anchor money, stated that as the measure embraced so many important considerations, it was not prepared at that time to give a definitive opinion on the subject.[54] Following the Treasury's decision, the governor issued a proclamation[55] on 21 August 1837 stating that the rates for the coins mentioned in the last proclamation (September 1836) would continue to be enforced until further notice. It included the coins mentioned in the September 1836 proclamation as well as the sterling copper penny, which was to pass at 1½d current money, and the copper halfpenny, which was to pass at ¾d (3 farthings).

The secretary of state, on 1 May 1838, requested information from the standing committee of West Indian planters and merchants in England on the difficulties which might arise because of the defective state of the monetary system in the West Indies when it became necessary to pay black labourers in money. The secretary of states made this request because of a petition made by the committee to the House of Commons.[56] The committee replied that the colonies had a right to a sound currency that rested on a metallic basis and to a sufficient supply of smaller coins. They recommended that the dollar and its fractional parts would be a convenient currency, since the coins already had an established relation to the money of account in the colonies and were well known to the labouring population.[57] The governor was also concerned that there would be a shortage of small coins which were required to pay the wages of the new labourers, but he was assured by the DCG that the latter held a large sum of British silver coins which could be made available in exchange for doubloons or dollars. However, the DCG did not believe that, at the rate of 4s 2d to the dollar and with the doubloon passing for $16, the silver coins would remain in circulation. Rather, he believed that they would be returned to the commissariat for the purchase of Treasury bills.[58]

At a public meeting, held on 6 September 1838, "for the purpose of considering the state of the Island Currency", it was agreed that any alteration in the relative value of coins then current in Barbados would interfere with all pending transactions between debtor and creditor; that the queen should be asked not to grant any further powers to the Colonial Bank; and that the most effectual legal mode to establish the present value of coins would be to convert currency into sterling by deducting one third, thus making the doubloon 66s 8d and the dollar 4s 2d. At the meeting, it was requested that the Honourable J.A. Beckles, president of the council, and Messrs Robert B. Clarke and John Bovell, members of the General Assembly for St Michael, submit the resolutions to their respective bodies.[59] The *Mercury* newspaper, which supported the Colonial Bank, was very critical of the meeting, especially the speech made by Mr Whitla, a respected merchant, who did not favour the bank. The *Liberal* newspaper, on the other hand, criticized the *Mercury* and the Colonial Bank.[60] Mr Clarke presented the resolutions to the House of Assembly, but then proceeded to criticize each resolution. He praised the Colonial Bank for bringing English capital to Barbados and stated that he had benefited from it. On the other hand, Mr Bovell severely criticized the bank.[61]

The experiment resulting from the 1825 proclamation was a failure. In addition to the problems already mentioned with the introduction of the British coins, in 1834 the DCG reported to the Treasury that, nine years after the proclamation, the British shilling was totally unknown in Barbados and most of the lower classes did not recognize it and regarded it as a foreign coin. Moreover, the British silver coins were, to a considerable extent, useless for the payment of the troops because the soldiers could not pass the coins in the markets except at a loss, on account of the value of the Spanish dollar at 4s 4d. As a result, none had been paid to the regiments in Barbados and St Lucia since the first remittances were received in 1825. The inconvenient fractions of the coins were not suited either to the other coins in circulation or to the money of account.[62] The main reasons for the failure are as follows:

1. Its uniform charge of 3 per cent commission on a London bill. The merchants and paymasters of the army found cheaper ways of transmitting funds to London; consequently, the circular flow of shillings into and out of the military chest did not materialize.

2. The Treasury's sterling parity with the Spanish dollar was incorrect because the old Elizabethan mint indenture of 1601 (5s 2d per ounce) had been used as the basis for the 1825 calculations but the mint price was then 2d per ounce above the market price. As a consequence, the Spanish dollar, at the rating of 4s 4d, was overvalued as against the shilling by about 3 per cent, and the shilling failed to become current.

3. There was a consequential error in rating doubloons. In the gold-using West Indies, the doubloon, then worth 64s sterling in intrinsic gold value, had long passed for 16 Spanish dollars. Thus, through the doubloon, there were local overvaluations of the Spanish dollar by some 9 per cent. The value of the doubloon was reduced in 1835 for army purposes to about 15¼ Spanish dollars, and the West Indies were driven off gold in the process.[63]

PROCLAMATION OF 1838

When it became evident that the British coins were not in circulation to the degree that had been anticipated, the committee of the Privy Council for coin was requested to decide whether British silver money or fractional parts of the dollar should be supplied to the West Indies. While the committee was still considering this matter, the Treasury issued instructions to the Mint to make enquiries in the market as to the quantity of silver bullion which could be provided and at what price, to enable the committee's decision to be effected immediately.[64] Governors were subsequently informed that the committee was preparing its report, and they should inform the legislatures and the public that they could be supplied with British silver coins by paying the Mint an equivalent in bullion, plus the usual charges of coinage.[65] Based on the report of the committee of the Privy Council for coin, an order in council of 7 September 1838 was made that revoked the order in council of 23 March 1825. A new currency rate was, thus, embodied in an order in council and a royal proclamation of 14 September 1838. The proclamation fixed the rates at which Spanish, Mexican and Columbian gold coins, called doubloons, and their silver coins, called dollars, should circulate and be received in the West India colonies. The doubloon was to circulate at 64s sterling and the dollar at 4s 2d sterling and to be taken as lawful tender in the same manner as if such tender had been made in the current coin of the United Kingdom.[66] The governor's proclamation, dated 26 October 1838,[67] stated that, as of 29 October 1838, all proclamations issued prior to that date were declared null and void and that the coins should be received and taken at the following rates of Barbados currency:

1. The doubloon at £5 and its fractional parts in the same proportion
2. The dollar at 6s 6d and its fractional parts in the same proportion
3. The British shilling at 1s 6d 3 farthings, and all other British silver coins and the fractional parts of the British shilling in the same proportion.

The DCG reported to the Treasury that there were objections to the proclamation from merchants and retail dealers in imported goods, who previously benefited from the rate of the doubloon, and by a few planters, but generally the principal mercantile businesses and planters were not openly hostile to it. The need for smaller coins to replace the fractional parts of the dollar was acute because British silver coins did not fit this purpose, owing to the difficult fractions involved with some of the smaller coins with which the black population had become accustomed. He suggested the halfpennies and farthings should be sent, as they were necessary to enable shillings and sixpences to pass for their proportionate parts of the dollar, and recommended that copper coins consisting of £100 in halfpennies and £20 in farthings be remitted. The ample stock of 1d pieces was almost useless because the lower classes were not convinced that 1d was equal to two halfpennies. He also suggested that £4,000 in fractional parts of the dollar should be sent to remove any inconvenience, but the Treasury did not approve this measure.[68]

There were several public meetings held after the publication of the local proclamation. The meetings were well attended and the petitions, signed by several persons, were sent to the secretary of state. The petitions were made by a wide cross-section of people: debtors and creditors; planters and merchants; supporters of the doubloon and supporters of the silver dollar; critics and supporters of the Colonial Bank. There was also a petition signed exclusively by merchants and another by planters. With respect to one of the petitions, the DCG reported to the Treasury that "although several of those who have put their names to it may be presumed not to understand the subject, there are others who must be perfectly aware what its effect would be if complied with, and who are nevertheless known to be debtors as proprietors or lessees".[69] The petitions were generally serious in their content, but one petitioner erroneously believed that the local proclamation was void because the queen was not in Barbados on the day it was issued. The governor informed the secretary of state that

> In the absence of Her Majesty's Solicitor General, who is at his country residence, I consider it right to mention that the learned gentleman appeared to experience some difficulty in drawing up the subsidiary Proclamation, published here, conformably with Your Lordship's directions, in the Queen's name; but the Sovereign is never deemed absent from Courts of Justice, and I presume, upon the like principle, that, in virtue, of the Royal Prerogative, Her Majesty's most gracious presence, may be legally held to pervade for all state purposes, every Possession under the dominion of the British Crown.[70]

One of the more important meetings "to protest the reduced value of the doubloon and the local currency and to consider alternative proposals" was chaired by Sir Reynold Alleyne (a planter and member of council) on 13 November 1838. At the meeting, it was agreed that coins would continue to be received and paid out at their current values. A committee was appointed to petition the queen to not grant the Colonial Bank further powers; and to request that currency debts be converted into sterling in such a way that equal justice would be done to both debtor and creditor. Pending a reply from the queen, other resolutions which were considered of a temporary nature were adopted at the meeting. The meeting considered that the money of account of Barbados should be kept either in British sterling or dollars, in order to remedy the inconvenience of keeping accounts in the island currency. If this suggestion were accepted, currency debts in dollars would be redeemed at the rate of 6s 3d to the dollar, but all currency debts which existed at the date the proclamation was issued, would be redeemed at 6s 6d, and debtors would have the option of paying debts contracted in doubloons at the rate of sixteen dollars each.[71] The queen's response to the petition was that she was pleased to receive it.[72] The Treasury stated that it "did not contemplate" any alteration in the comparative values that had been assigned to the gold and silver coins in circulation in the West Indian colonies.[73]

A petition from planters in December 1838 reflected their special problems. They were concerned that there would be a deficiency of small coins, since no action had been taken to coin the fractional parts of the dollar at the Mint for circulation in the colonies. The planters attributed the shortage to the difference between the nominal and intrinsic relative currency value at which the doubloon and the dollar passed in Barbados. They were of the opinion that the value of the doubloon should remain unchanged, but that the dollar should be fixed at 6s 6d. On account of the sudden abolition of the apprenticeship system and since the supply of small silver coins could not be obtained immediately, they suggested that, in order to meet the demand for wages, the governor, for a limited period, should permit the circulation of British shillings and sixpences as the fractional parts of a dollar at the rate of one quarter dollar to the shilling.

When the draft order in council confirming the governor's proclamation was sent to the office of the Privy Council, the law officers of the Crown pointed out that, according to the queen's proclamation, the dollar should have been rated at 6s 6⅛ d currency whereas the governor's proclamation fixed it at 6s 6d currency.[74] After the exchange of several letters between the colonial office, the office of the Privy Council and the Treasury,[75] the Treasury confirmed that it was aware of the difference, but that the governor's computation was done at its suggestion and the small difference was not likely to produce inconvenience.⁷⁶ The governor's proclamation was confirmed by an order in council on 11 July 1839. He was informed that "the several Memorials and Representations from Planters and other parties at Barbados were duly referred for the consideration and decision of the Lords Commissioners of the Treasury, but that they have not appeared to their Lordships to call for any modification of the directions given by Her Majesty's Government on the question of the Currency".⁷⁷

The *Barbadian* on 24 August 1839 expressed the following views on the order in council in an editorial:

> At last, to the great annoyance of this community that wicked, abominable, and perplexing currency, 6s. 6d. to the dollar, is forced upon us. Her Majesty the Queen, who we dare say knows as much about currency matters as We do, has been advised by her ministers to add the seal of her royal confirmation to the Proclamation for establishing this rate of Currency issued by His Excellency the Governor in October last, in the name of the Queen; but which Proclamation it appears was denied here to be valid, without her Majesty's express sanction, and which was indeed declared to be of no validity by her majesty's own Attorney General, whose opinion our public spirited townsman, Mr. Whitla, went to the trouble and expense to obtain from England. This opinion was published lately in the Globe paper. The matter is not set at rest. Six shillings and six pence currency is the established value of the dollar. But how is the dollar to be divided? How many pence and farthings to the bitt and half-bitt? What is the 16th of a dollar, the five penny piece as we call it? – four pence three farthings and a fraction. Oh! it is abominable! But why be bothered about any currency at all, at all? Let every one deal in dollars and cents. That is the only alternative which our poor foolish head can think of. In our books we have abolished pounds, shillings and pence altogether; and we render our accounts in dollars and cents. Trouble is a thing we hate, and this mode of keeping accounts saves us a deal of trouble.

Some British silver coins were not convenient because of the differences in the money of account in the West Indies. When a consignment of 4d and 2d pieces was sent to the commissariat in 1839, the DCG informed the Treasury that they were useful in several of the colonies, because they corresponded to the subdivisions of the dollar and the small coins previously in use among the blacks, but in other colonies they did not circulate. He, therefore, requested a further supply of £5,000 in shillings and half-crowns for those stations.⁷⁸

The Colonial Bank in 1840 told the Treasury that it was prepared to supply dollars or other specie for the public service in the West Indies and Canada. No agreement was reached because the terms offered by the Colonial Bank were more expensive than when the Treasury directly supplied the commissariats.[79] However, in 1845 the Treasury agreed that the Colonial Bank would supply the commissariat chests in the Windward and Leeward command with specie not exceeding £200,000 between 1 June 1845 and 1 June 1846.[80] During the period June 1847 to August 1849, however, there was no agreement because of the war between the United States and Mexico. At this time, the Treasury supplied the commissariat with the money required.

The problem of different monies of account in the West Indies and the scarcity of small coins persisted. The Treasury, in December 1847, sent to the commissariat in Barbados £40,000 in British coins: £20,000 in gold, of which £4,000 were in half-sovereigns; and £20,000 in silver, of which £8,000 were half-crowns, £5,000 were shillings and £7,000 were sixpences.[81] However, on account of a great scarcity of small coins in Barbados, the Treasury instructed the Mint to ship immediately to the commissariat £3,500 worth of British coins consisting of £1,500 in fourpenny pieces, £1,000 in threepenny pieces in new silver coins, and in copper coins £500 in one penny pieces and £500 in halfpenny pieces. The DCG was authorized to issue these coins to the government in exchange for an equivalent amount in any coins which were admissible in the transaction of his chest.[82] When the coins arrived in Barbados, the governor was made aware that many persons refused to accept them, except at a discount. The following government notice was issued:

> One Dollar is equal to 100 Cents or 4 shillings and 2 pence;
>
> Half Dollar is equal to 50 Cents or 2 shillings and 1 penny;
>
> Quarter Dollar is equal to 25 Cents or 1 shilling and a half penny;
>
> One-eighth of a Dollar (commonly called a bit and 2 pence) is equal to 12½ cents or 6 pence and 1 farthing;
>
> Four penny pieces equal to 8 cents each;
>
> Three penny pieces equal to 6 cents each;
>
> Copper pennies equal to 2 cents each;
>
> Copper half penny equal to 1 cent each;
>
> Copper farthing equal to half a cent each.[83]

The florin (2s) was made legal tender in 1849 and the coinage of the half-crown was discontinued until 1874 in order to give the florin a fair trial.

ASSIMILATION OF THE CURRENCY

The policy of the British government related not only to which foreign coins should be considered legal tender in the colonies and the rates at which they should be accepted, but also to the mode in which the government accounts should be kept. In 1845, an act was passed "authorising the Vestries to keep their accounts in dollars and cents". The governor suggested its disallowance because of the inconvenience likely to result from adopting that system.[84] The act was disallowed, on the recommendation of the Treasury, on the grounds that the currency of account in the colonies should be assimilated to that of the United Kingdom; and that the assessment of public dues should not be made in a denomination not coined by the Mint and liable to variations of intrinsic value. The secretary of state agreed that it was desirable that calculations in sterling be substituted for "island currency" in colonial acts.[85] In the same year, the Export and Import Duty Act, for the first time, stated the duties in dollars and cents instead of pounds, shillings and pence. The secretary of state did not disallow the act, but instructed the governor not to give his assent to any future legislation in which the same objectionable method of account might be followed.[86]

An unsuccessful attempt was made in the House of Assembly in 1835 to assimilate the currency of Barbados with that of Great Britain.[87] Between 1839 and early in 1848, further attempts were also made. The inconvenience and problems created by the money of account were eventually settled by Act No. 1 of 21 August 1848, which provided for the assimilation of the currency and moneys of account of Barbados to that of the United Kingdom of Great Britain and Ireland. It stated that, as of the commencement of the act, public and parochial receipts and payments would be converted into sterling money and the public accounts would be kept in that currency at the rate of £100 sterling for £156 currency of Barbados. The last section of the act stated: "Nothing in this Act contained shall be construed to interfere with the circulation of any foreign coins, which by Her Majesty's Proclamation now or shall hereafter be declared current in this Island, at such value in the currency of the United Kingdom as now or shall hereafter be fixed by any such Proclamation or Proclamations."

3

The Advent of the Banks

BANKING REGULATIONS

Prior to the enactment of Sir Robert Peel's bank acts of 1844 to 1845, the banks which had been established in the colonies were governed by the grant of royal charters or by colonial acts of incorporation. The chancellor of the exchequer, in November 1831, was concerned that royal charters were being granted to banking companies. He stated that it was of the highest public importance that these charters should be framed upon a settled and consistent principle, and argued that the desired result could not be attained if they were granted indiscriminately by various independent departments without reference to the Treasury. He suggested to the secretaries of state for the Home Department, the colonies and the Privy Council for Trade that, before entertaining an application for a charter, the Treasury's opinion should be obtained.[1] In April 1833, the Treasury drafted rules relating to the grant of charters to banking companies either in England or overseas and suggested that, before a decision was taken on an application, it should be referred to the Board of Trade so that a distinct report could be obtained both on its merits and on the provisions to be included in the charter.[2]

By 1838, a banking policy regarding the issue of notes evolved with the following aims. It

1. Required that notes be cashed on demand in specie at the place of issue, as well as at the principal establishments of the issuing banks;
2. Prevented the issue of notes under £1 currency;
3. Insisted on the publication of periodic returns of assets and liabilities, as an indication to the public of the financial position of banks of issue; and
4. Safeguarded issues by making shareholders liable for twice the amount of their shares.

When some colonial acts for incorporating banks failed to meet these standards, the Colonial Office asked the Treasury and the Board of Trade on 7 January 1839 "to draw up an abstract of such Regulations as they may think indispensable, in order that they may be transmitted to the Colonial Possessions of the Crown for the information and guidance of the Governors and Legislative Bodies in those Colonies".[3] The regulations were communicated to the colonies by Lord John Russell's circular of 4 May 1840 and were revised in 1846 "with a view to bring them into exact accordance with the principles on these subjects established in this country". (See appendix 3.)

As a result of problems arising from some banks in the colonies, it was decided in 1853 that, since the Treasury was responsible for all financial matters connected with the colonies, in future, all applications relating exclusively to bank charters should be sent to the Treasury, which would be solely responsible for the settlement of the conditions on which charters of banking companies in the colonies should be granted.[4]

THE COLONIAL BANK

In the Emancipation Act of 1833, the British government was authorized to pay slave owners in the colonies substantial sums in compensation for freeing their slaves. At that time, the demands of West Indian planters for finance from the merchant bankers in Great Britain were becoming more extensive, and the local merchants and moneylenders were unable to provide such credit. This need for finance was especially great in Trinidad and British Guiana where the sugar industry was rapidly expanding.

It was against this background that a group of merchants and private bankers in England conceived the plan to establish a bank with its head office in London and branches in the West Indies and British Guiana. By 1836, when their negotiations had reached the point where they could proceed to call up capital, the period of prosperity in England had passed but they decided to continue with their venture.[5] The Colonial Bank was incorporated on 1 June 1836 by a royal charter for a period of twenty years, commencing 1 May 1836. Its purpose was to provide banking services only in Jamaica, other West Indian colonies and British Guiana. The nominal capital was £2 million, divided in twenty thousand shares of £100 each. However, the Colonial Bank could not commence business until £1.5 million had been subscribed and £500,000 had been actually paid up. Three thousand shares were to be allotted to persons resident in the West Indies; however, after six months, any of the unsubscribed shares could be allocated to persons in the United Kingdom. The shareholders would only be liable for the amount of their subscription.

Under the charter, the Colonial Bank was permitted to carry on the business of bankers by dealing generally in bullion, money and bills of exchange, and by lending money on commercial paper and government securities, doing so in such lawful ways and means as were usually practised among bankers. However, the bank could not lend or advance money on the security of lands, houses or tenements or upon ships, nor deal in goods, wares or merchandise of any nature or kind whatsoever. It was empowered to establish one or more principal bank or banks in Jamaica and Barbados and in other places in the West Indies and British Guiana; to set up branches or agencies; and to make, issue and circulate notes payable in dollars to bearer on demand at the place where the notes were issued, provided that no note should be issued for less than $5. The notes were to be paid in dollars of acknowledged weight and fineness to bearer on demand, as well as at such principal bank or banks, and every of them, as at the branch or agency from which the same had been issued. (The places at which these notes could be redeemed were later disputed by the Colonial Bank.) At the end of twenty years, the Colonial Bank's business would be wound up. There was no limitation in the charter on the Colonial Bank's note issue, and no stipulation that it be secured in any way. In the draft charter, the Colonial Bank had proposed to establish offices in Canada, Nova Scotia and the other British colonies in the North American continent, but the Colonial Office did not agree to this proposal.[6]

In August 1836, the Colonial Bank asked the Mint to coin, on its behalf, 5¢, 10¢, 25¢ and 50¢ in silver and 1¢ in copper for use in the West Indies.[7]

The Treasury and the Privy Council for Trade agreed on the understanding that their permission was not to be considered as giving any authorized currency to the coins or conveying any sanction for their substitution at the Colonial Bank's option for the dollars then in circulation. Neither did it imply any intention on the part of the British government to give the coins any legalized currency or value in circulation beyond what they might acquire under local laws. The Colonial Bank was also told that the weight and fineness of its tokens should be the same as the dollar and that the coins should indicate their origin, such as with the inscription "Colonial Bank Tokens". Also, the bank would be responsible for their redemption by paying the public in the same dollars in which it was bound to pay its notes.[8] The Colonial Bank did not proceed with the minting of the coins because of the imposition of these conditions.[9] In June 1837, the bank again applied (this time, unsuccessfully) to the Treasury for the Mint to coin, on its behalf, 1¢ pieces in copper or mixed metal and 5¢, 10¢ and 20¢ pieces in silver.[10]

The secretary of state, in November 1836, informed governors that, while the charter did not confer any exclusive privileges on the Colonial Bank, the British government would not grant a charter to another bank in the West Indies until the Colonial Bank had an opportunity to establish itself; they should, therefore, not assent to a law for the establishment of a new bank without his consent. However, the secretary of state postponed his decision on whether government's funds should be deposited in the Colonial Bank until the bank could show that it was a safe and convenient place to deposit the public's money.[11]

On 1 May 1837, Michael M'Chlery, manager of the Head Bank at Barbados and superintendent of its branches, issued the following notice:

> The Colonial Bank will commence business in this Island simultaneously with Branches established in British Guiana and Trinidad on the 15th day of May, instant. The following are the terms on which the Bank will transact business.
>
> **General Terms of Business**
>
> Local Bills and Bills of Hand bearing two or more approved names, will be discounted at the rate of 5 to 6 per cent per annum, according to the time they have to run. No Bills having more than nine months to run will be discounted.
>
> Cash Credits will be granted to parties on their Bond, jointly with two or more approved Securities, at the rate of 5 per cent per annum on the sum in advance, and a moderate charge for keeping the accounts.

Specie and Foreign Bills of Exchange will be received and supplied at a fair and reasonable rate, having reference to the value of money in Great Britain and America, and other Countries, with a view of facilitating remittances between the West Indies, British America, Europe &.

Inter-Colonial Bills and Orders will be granted to parties transmitting money from one Branch to another at a moderate charge.

Deposits will be received by the Bank for which interest will be allowed according to the amount and time deposited.

Current Deposit Accounts will be opened with the Merchants, and others desirous of having their money and cash accounts kept at the Bank for their convenience and security. It is expected that depositors shall always keep a respectable balance in the Bank, or if preferred, these accounts will be kept at a moderate per centage.

Notes will be issued by the Bank for sums not less than five dollars. These notes are payable on demand in silver dollars, or should the holder prefer it he may be accommodated with other equivalent current Coin, Bills of Exchange on London, America, or Inter-Colonial Orders.

The Accounts of the Bank will be kept in dollars and cents.

Blank Cheques and Bank Books will be supplied by the Bank.

Hours of Business 10 till 2.

NB. Punctuality in money transactions is one of the fundamental principles in all Banking Establishments, and it is of vital importance to the well being of every institution of this description; and the strictest regularity in the punctual payment of all Bills, or other engagements between the Public and the Bank, will be expected and invariably enforced.[12]

In May 1837, the collector of customs enquired whether he should receive the notes of the Colonial Bank in payment of customs duties. He was advised by the Barbados solicitor general that he was required by the Letters Patent to accept them, but this decision was subsequently revoked by the British Treasury.[13] Later in the year, the Colonial Bank proposed that its notes should be received in payment of duties and taxes by government departments and that the bank could be used for the deposit of public monies in the West Indies, but this proposal was also rejected by the Colonial Office and the Treasury.[14] Governors were informed that the Treasury had "advised caution against any proceedings which might imply that the British government considered the notes to be legal or authorized tender . . . on any other ground than the confidence [which] individuals ... [might] feel in the credit of the [bank], and the ready convertibility on demand of its notes into specie".[15]

In July 1838, the Colonial Bank complained to the Committee for Trade regarding the issue of notes by the indigenous banks in Jamaica and British Guiana. The bank asked that it be permitted to redeem its notes in dollars or doubloons or the currency of the place where such notes might be presented for payment, but the request was denied.[16] Following the 1838 proclamation, the Colonial Bank was granted a supplementary charter on 30 October 1838, which permitted it to redeem its notes in any currency which was legal tender in the West Indian colonies, that is, in United Kingdom coins, Spanish, Mexican and Columbian silver dollars and gold coins.

The Colonial Bank was not supported by all sections of the community. When it was granted a supplementary charter, the following petition was sent to the queen:

> Your Petitioners have further most respectfully to submit to Your Majesty that notwithstanding there was an abundance of Gold Coins in this Island for internal and external trade, a number of wealthy capitalists in London projected a Company designed "The Colonial Bank" who obtained a Royal Charter from Your immediate predecessor William 4th of blessed memory, with powers to issue bank notes, that many of Your Petitioners believe all writers on political economy concur that in a country where there is a sufficiency of the precious metals to carry on the functions of trade the intervention of paper money displaces a like quantity of metallic currency, out of the country ... and as dealers in money with a large capital and many branches such as the Colonial Bank, gives it the power of withdrawing from circulation a large portion of the silver coins when there is a prospect of gain by exporting it ... We Your humble Petitioners therefore most earnestly pray Your Majesty may not grant any further powers to the Colonial Bank.[17]

The reply to the petition was that the British government "did not contemplate any extension of the privileges or alteration" in the charter.[18]

In January 1839, there was a rumour that the Colonial Bank intended to establish an agency in Cuba where slavery still existed. The bank explained that it had no intention to promote the African slave trade and that the agency was only a means of facilitating their transactions in the colonies.[19] The law officers of the Crown advised that the charter authorized the Colonial Bank to carry on the business of banking "in Jamaica and the other West India Islands and not elsewhere", and that the proposed agency would violate the terms of the charter, which might be repealed.[20] However, in May 1837 the Colonial Bank had received the following opinion from their legal advisers:

> We think that it would be competent to the Colonial Bank to establish banks or agencies in places in the West Indies not within the British dominions and in other foreign countries not in the West Indies provided they are not precluded from so doing by the laws or Governments of those countries. If the establishing of such branches in foreign countries should be considered as contrary to the terms imposed by the Charter on the Colonial Bank (which however we do not think the case) the Crown might take proceedings to annul the Charter.

The Colonial Bank did not establish the agency because it appeared that the Government of Spain would not grant them permission to do so.[21]

The difference in legal opinions occurred because the preamble of the charter stated that "the shareholders have united together to establish banks of issue and deposit in the West Indies and British Guiana and elsewhere"; however, the charter also stated "not elsewhere subject to such restrictions and provisions as are hereinafter contained". It was claimed that the words "and elsewhere" were a clerical error which was detected after the charter had received the great seal, but the restrictions were clear that the Colonial Bank could establish offices only in the West Indies and British Guiana.

In November 1840, the Colonial Bank applied for another supplementary charter to issue notes in sterling.[22] While the views of the Committee for Trade and the Treasury were being obtained, a John Innes informed the secretary of state that the Colonial Bank was in violation of its charter, as it had issued notes in Venezuela and St Thomas.[23] At the request of the Committee for Trade, action on the application was suspended pending an explanation from the bank.[24] The directors of the bank did not see the need to justify its proceedings to Innes or any other private individual, as they opened the banks in those countries and issued notes there based on the legal opinion given by two eminent lawyers in 1837.[25] The matter was referred to the law officers of the Crown who advised that the bank had violated its charter by establishing banks in those countries and that "the Crown never could have been advised to grant a charter to the Company to establish Banks all over the world".[26] A supplementary charter was not granted, but the bank issued a note for £1 0s 10d sterling, which was equivalent to $5, and it also included the equivalent amount in currency and in dollars.

Act No. 1 of 1841 authorized the enrolment in the Colonial Secretary's Office copies of the Colonial Bank's charter and supplemental charter to render the same, or certified copies as evidence in the law courts. Subsequently, several local acts authorized the deposit of government balances in the Colonial Bank as well as the deposit of funds by some private institutions.

When the charter was due to expire, the Colonial Bank in 1855 applied for a supplementary charter to prolong its powers, but the law officers advised that there was no provision in the original charter for an extension and that it could not be extended without the consent of all the existing shareholders. The Colonial Bank withdrew its application because of the difficulty in securing such consent and instead obtained a Private Act (9 Vict. Cap. III) of 1856. The act eliminated the twenty-year period, but the shareholders were given the power to continue or discontinue the business of the bank at two general meetings specifically called for that purpose. The act authorized the bank to issue, in the West Indies and British Guiana but not elsewhere, sterling notes of not less than £1 and multiples of the pound payable in current money of the United Kingdom, or in other coins legally current in the colonies. Notes issued in dollars should be payable either in Spanish or Mexican dollars, or in British money at the rate of 4s 2d British money to the dollar. The Colonial Bank was also given limited powers to take and hold land or other real or personal estate temporarily for debts due to it. The liabilities of the bank could not exceed three times the amount of the paid-up capital and it was required to keep a reserve in specie or gold and silver bullion amounting to at least one-third the value of its note circulation, which would be verified by quarterly returns to the Treasury and by its inspection. The records of the Colonial Bank in the islands could be inspected by the governments, with the permission of the Treasury, but this practice where it existed was discontinued in 1884. It is interesting to note that the returns required by the act were not sent by the Colonial Bank to the Treasury.[27]

Abortive attempts were made in 1887 and 1889 to amend the act. However, the Colonial Bank Act of 1898 altered and extended the constitution and powers of the bank, which, inter alia:

1. Converted twenty thousand shares of £100 each into one hundred thousand shares of £20 each, of which £6 were deemed to have been paid up;
2. Applied certain provisions of the Companies Acts of 1845 and 1863 to the bank;

3. Authorized the continuance of the offices established in England and New York for the purpose of facilitating, originating or completing operations directly connected with the bank's business only in the West Indies and British Guiana, and, with the Treasury's consent, the establishment of other offices for similar purposes, but not for any other purpose;
4. Fixed the maximum note circulation of the bank to an amount not exceeding £500,000 subject to agreement between it and the Treasury, and deposit coin or securities of not less than 25 per cent of its notes in circulation with the Crown agents or trustees appointed by the Treasury;
5. Made the uncalled capital, in the event of winding up, satisfy the demands of note holders in priority to other claims;
6. Ensured that a colonial legislature would not have the power to interfere with the constitution of the bank, but that the bank was otherwise subject to colonial law;
7. Relieved the Treasury of certain duties imposed by the 1856 act and made further provision for the security of holders of notes issued by the bank.

In January 1899, the Colonial Bank in Barbados was directed by the British Treasury to deposit £15,000 in coin in its vault for the security of its note issue. The Treasury then appointed the colonial secretary and the colonial treasurer as trustees for the coin deposited. A Board of Survey, consisting of the colonial secretary, the colonial treasurer and the bank manager, was appointed to inspect the specie. However, in May, with the approval of the British Treasury, the Colonial Bank deposited £15,000 in stock with the Crown's agents in lieu of the coin deposited in Barbados, and from that date the securities were deposited only with the Crown's agents.[28]

THE WEST INDIA BANK

Prior to the establishment of the West India Bank, a prospectus was published in the *Globe* newspaper on 22 November 1838 for the establishment of a bank, to be called the Barbados Bank, with a capital of £200,000 divided in 5,000 of £40 each. However, the capital was not raised and the Barbados Bank was not established. In September 1839, a prospectus was issued in Barbados for the establishment of a commercial bank on joint stock principles in the island, with branches in other islands and agents in Great Britain, British America, the United States and St Thomas. There was favourable reaction to the proposal of a bank in Barbados and in some of the other islands where the prospectus was published. The first meeting of local subscribers, mainly planters and merchants, was held on 28 November 1839. There, extraordinary directors were appointed and invested with authority to devise some practical plan to commence operations in Barbados on 1 February 1840 or as soon as possible. Arising from a meeting of these directors, a petition was sent to the queen in January 1840 with the request that the petitioners be granted letters patent or a charter of incorporation to establish a bank of issue, loan and deposit in the West Indies and British Guiana.[29]

Pending the receipt of a royal charter, a deed of settlement was entered into so that the West India Bank could commence business. The deed provided that the shares of the bank would be twenty thousand shares of $100 each, of which five thousand shares would be allocated to Barbados, and it also included provisions for the mode of appointment of extraordinary directors and the court of directors.[30] The West India Bank began business in Barbados on 2 March 1840 and, during the year, branches were established in Trinidad, St Vincent, Antigua, Grenada, St Kitts, Nevis and Tobago, and agents were appointed in Demerara, Dominica, St Lucia, Jamaica, St Thomas, New York and London.[31]

A royal charter was granted on 27 November 1840. It provided, inter alia, that, with effect from 1 January 1841, the West India Bank could, for a period of twenty-one years, issue and circulate notes of not less than $5 within the islands, but it could not lend or advance money on the security of land, houses, and so on. The West India Bank could not begin operations under the charter until $1 million was subscribed and $500,000 actually paid up. The whole capital of $2 million was to be paid up within two years of the grant of the charter.

The antagonism by the Colonial Bank of the West India Bank was expected, since the two banks were in direct competition for customers. As early as May 1840, the manager of the Colonial Bank in Trinidad was directed by the head office in London to make arrangements in Barbados for a weekly exchange of notes between the two banks, with the balance payable in silver dollars.[32] Later in the year, the Trinidad manager was instructed by the head office that he was not to accept the West India Bank's notes; that he should not afford accommodation to persons who were the originators and supporters of the rival bank; and that he should insist on payment from them as well as doubtful customers so that they might transfer their accounts to the West India Bank.[33]

When the West India Bank was unable to raise the paid-up capital as required by the charter, it petitioned the secretary of state in November 1842 to dispense with the condition that the capital of $2 million be paid up within two years. In lieu, it asked the secretary of state to substitute a condition requiring $1 million paid up and the remainder of the capital to be paid up within four years, and asked that the directors be empowered to call for the remainder from time to time as its business became more extended and could find employment for the capital. The petition was supported by the governor, but the Treasury was of the opinion that, since the West India Bank had not complied with the conditions of the charter, it would have to produce satisfactory evidence with regard to the period for completing the remaining amount of subscription and capital.[34]

In addition to paying interest on fixed deposits, the West India Bank paid interest at the rate of 2½ per cent on current accounts, which tended to draw customers away from the Colonial Bank. However, the Colonial Bank decided that it would not pay interest on current accounts on the grounds that the West India Bank would soon overburden itself with these deposits on which it had to pay interest, and without the adequate means of employing the capital.[35] This decision was prophetic because, on 31 December, the West India Bank ceased to pay interest on current accounts.

In June 1845, at the instigation of the Colonial Bank, the secretary of state drew the governor's attention to the fact that the paid-up capital of the West India Bank at 31 August 1844 was $529,700 and at 28 February 1845 was $530,200 although the charter required that the capital of $2 million should have been paid in full on 27 November 1842.[36] The directors of the West India Bank explained that people in the West Indies were not experienced in raising large sums by joint stock and that many shareholders, fearing that the charter might be terminated, offered their shares for sale. They also pointed out that the population in the territories in which the West India Bank operated was only 320,318 and that the paid-up capital should be viewed in some proportion to the population and to the prospect for circulation. The directors suggested that the provision requiring that the whole of the capital be paid up should be rescinded. The governor supported these views and added that the accommodation afforded by the two banks, especially by the easier system of the West India Bank, was a main agent in sustaining, reviving and extending the cultivation and the manufacture of sugar and the retail trades of all descriptions in Barbados and the neighbouring islands.[37] The Treasury, while agreeing with these observations, remarked in part that the directors should have been aware of these facts when the application was made for the charter. However, as the West India Bank had performed a useful function, the Treasury would be prepared, in the event of the revocation of the charter, to recommend the grant of a new charter upon such amount of capital as the directors felt warranted in applying for, subject to the absolute conditions for subscription and payment of the whole in full without delay, but with a proviso for further increasing the capital at a future date.[38]

The West India Bank appointed a committee in April 1846 to negotiate with the Colonial Office in England for either an amendment of the existing charter or a new charter. The committee proposed that the bank be granted a supplementary charter with a capital of $600,000 in shares of $50 and that the whole of the capital be subscribed and paid up within four months of the date of the new charter. The advice given to the Treasury was that it was very doubtful whether, in the event that the charter were revoked, the directors, acting on behalf of the shareholders, could accept a new charter to make the new conditions and liabilities legally binding upon the existing shareholders, and also whether the liabilities and assets of the company under the present charter could be transferred to a new corporation and be legally binding both upon the new corporation and on the debtors of the existing company. However, on account of the usefulness of the West India Bank to the economies of Barbados and the other West Indian colonies, the Treasury abstained from advising the queen to revoke the charter, notwithstanding that it had deviated from the charter. This course was adopted with the distinct understanding that the future proceedings of the West India Bank should be strictly regulated by the paid-up capital only.[39]

Towards the end of November 1847, a rumour circulated in Barbados that the West India Bank was unable to redeem its notes and that persons holding them were likely to suffer a loss. It was alleged that the bank had run short of silver, which had been withdrawn by the merchants to purchase the commissariat's bills that had been receiving tenders below the rates of the banks. A run was made on the West India Bank and some persons took advantage of the situation by purchasing the notes at a discount.[40] On 1 December 1847, it was reported that the West India Bank was entirely drained of its specie and was obliged to suspend payment. The planters, who in many instances depended on credit from the bank, were unable to procure dollars to make the weekly payment to their labourers and it was expected that they would have serious difficulties in paying for labour especially at the commencement of the crop.[41] The mercantile community in Barbados and in some of the islands tried to maintain confidence in the notes of the West India Bank. They rallied in support of the bank by offering to receive the notes as usual for the purchase of goods and settlement of accounts, allowing a liberal discount for prompt payment.[42] When news of the West India Bank's failure reached Trinidad, there was a run on the bank and, after several days, it was compelled to decline specie payments for its notes. However, merchants continued to receive the bank's notes in payment of outstanding accounts.[43]

The situation was exacerbated by the failure of the Royal Bank of Liverpool, which brought ruin to several mercantile firms in that city including the firm of Barton, Irlam and Higginson, West Indian merchants with whom half of the planters in Barbados were connected. The *Barbadian* newspaper stated:

> [T]his blow upon the House of Barton, Irlam and Higginson will be felt in every fibre of our mercantile and agricultural body. It is impossible to describe the panic amongst our citizens, and the distress visible in every countenance – the gloom will pervade the whole Island. It is difficult to say how many families indeed will be affected by the misfortune which has fallen upon a House intimately connected with this Island.[44]

The *Barbadian Globe* reported, on 6 December, that in the present monetary crisis which had fallen on Barbados, the labourers had conducted themselves in the most exemplary and praiseworthy manner. On several estates, the workers voluntarily offered to accept 12½¢ for their day's labour, and on other estates they asked their employers to give them food in lieu of a certain amount of wages and they would cheerfully wait for the balance in cash until such time as specie became plentiful in the colony.

The secretary of state was informed that the West India Bank had suspended payment and that the surplus of Barbados was deposited in that bank. He was told that the government had been thrown into a state of embarrassment, compounded by the failure of the House of Higginson and Co. of Liverpool with whom half of the planters of the island were connected. The result was that wages had ceased to be paid and retail trade virtually suspended. However, the labourers had behaved well and were either at work for provisions as part wages or in their own gardens. The Colonial Bank contracted its operations to meet these difficulties. Among the deposits in that bank was a sum of between £2,000 and £3,000 from the colonial share for the erection of the Barbados lighthouse, but the governor gave instructions that the money should not be withdrawn because that action might have led to a suspension of payment by the Colonial Bank. Nothwithstanding a run on the Colonial Bank, its notes were paid in coin, but it could neither discount the bills of the planters nor make advances for the payment of wages. In order not to cause discontent among the police, the commanding officer of the forces was requested to pay them from the military chest.[45]

The local shareholders met on 8 December and appointed a committee to examine the state of the West India Bank's affairs. The committee reported that

1. It would not have been necessary to suspend specie payment if the bank had strictly adhered to legitimate banking operations.
2. The reasons given by the manager and the secretary of the bank for the suspension of specie payment were inconsistent.
3. Large accommodation, principally of a local nature, was afforded to some individuals who were already heavily indebted to the bank, in spite of repeated warnings to the manager by the board of directors.
4. The directors were granted large cash credits which, in many instances, were not beneficial to the bank.
5. The manager had allowed many accounts to a very considerable amount to be overdrawn, and among those were the accounts of the manager, the secretary and the cashier.
6. Bills amounting to £60,500 sterling drawn on the bankrupt firm of Barton, Irlam and Higginson passed through the Barbados branch, a portion of which was drawn by Higginson, Deane and Stott, and without endorsers.

The committee concluded that if debts were collected, cash credits were reduced, a different system of management were adopted, and a commission were appointed to supervise the establishment, there was no reason why the West India Bank could not resume operations. However, these observations related only to the Barbados branch. It considered that no decisive measures should be taken until the next general meeting of the extraordinary directors, when reports from the other branches would be available.

A detailed report from the court of directors on the West India Bank's affairs, as at 27 November 1847, was given at the meeting of the extraordinary directors, held on 5 January 1848. The financial position is shown in table 3.1.

Table 3.1 Financial Position of the West India Bank, 27 November 1847

Territory	Assets ($)		
	Total Apparent	Good Debts	Apparent Bad Debts
Trinidad	563,377	461,442	101,935
Grenada	176,698	142,254	34,444
St Vincent	156,590	151,530	5,060
Antigua	185,881	185,881	–
St Kitts	104,723	83,518	21,205
Nevis	81,687	78,515	3,172
Tobago	37,350	37,350	–
Barbados	767,282	678,511	88,771
Total	2,073,588	1,819,001	254,587

The committee's assessment of the management of the branches was that Antigua and Tobago were very satisfactory. The conduct of the present manager of Trinidad was most reprehensible because he made loans to himself and his firm, of which 62 per cent was totally uncovered by security. The conduct of the Grenada manager was also most reprehensible because he had granted himself and his family connections the majority of the bad debts. The St Vincent manager had not exercised ordinary caution by permitting so large an amount of irregular transactions to take place, contrary to the instructions and regulations of the West India Bank. Bad debts on one transaction by the former manager of the St Kitts branch were most irregular and reprehensible. The conduct of the Nevis manager was irregular and unwarrantable because he had made advances on cash accounts without obeying the instructions of the directors. Astonishment and dismay were expressed at the conduct of the Barbados manager who had habitually disregarded the rules and regulations in spite of the warnings by the directors, and notwithstanding the repeated disapproval of the directors, he not only continued to overdraw his account but increased it. In addition, he had made irregular advances to others. The committee had no confidence in the Barbados manager and recommended that he be removed immediately. It also passed a vote of no confidence on the cashier and recommended that the managers of the several branches should be directed to suspend the issue of notes.[46]

In January 1848, there were meetings of depositors and other claimants and also of shareholders. The latter meeting resulted in the expulsion of two directors, for irregular transactions with the West India Bank, as well as the manager and cashier. It was also recommended that the secretary be dismissed immediately since he had forfeited their confidence. When it became evident that it would be difficult to carry on business, the chairman of the board of directors petitioned Her Majesty in February 1848 to revoke the royal charter and to grant the West India Bank the power to resume its ordinary banking business if, on winding up their affairs, the queen found such resumption advisable.[47] The West India Bank never resumed business.

A notice was published by the West India Bank in April 1848 stating that the first instalment of $5 per share of a call of $15 on the shareholders was due on 12 April and that those persons who had not paid up the respective amounts were required to do so forthwith with interest at the rate of 6 per cent per annum, in default of which immediate steps would be taken to enforce the same.[48] One of the last notices regarding the West India Bank appeared in February 1850. It stated that subscribers (Barrow and Dummett) held a large amount of the West India Bank's paper, which they would dispose of at a liberal discount.[49]

The West India Bank paid dividends during the whole period of its existence. A comparison of the dividends paid by the West India Bank and the Colonial Bank is as follows:

Year	West India Bank	Colonial Bank
	(%)	
1840	6	8
1841	6	5
1842	6	3
1843	7	3
1844	8	–
1845	8	–
1846	8	2
1847	8	2

The West India Bank was truly a West Indian institution, with indigenous shareholders and with branches in most of the British West Indian colonies. During its period of existence, it performed a very useful function. Its lending policies, particularly to the agricultural and distributive sectors, assisted in the development of the economy of the colonies. The West India Bank was also innovative with respect to the payment of interest on current accounts; in addition, it was not as conservative as the Colonial Bank in its lending policies.

There were several factors which contributed to its demise. The report of the Committee of Inspection documented serious cases of mismanagement by the managers and other officers as well as their bad judgement in making loans to themselves and their associates, without obtaining adequate security. It would appear that the extraordinary directors and the court of directors did not perform their duties in a professional manner. The main problem was the capitalization of the West India Bank, because it was too ambitious in expecting that a capital of $2 million could be raised, and was dilatory in seeking an amendment to its charter when it became evident that this could not be achieved. External factors, such as the passing of the English Sugar Duties Act of 1846 to equalize the tariff on sugar, led to a severe reduction in the price of sugar. After the passing of this act, a commercial crisis occurred in England which plunged into bankruptcy, in that country, a number of merchants who had, in the past, provided credit for the Barbadian planters and merchants. The greatest shock to Barbados was the failure of the Royal Bank of Liverpool and the firm of Barton, Irlam and Higginson, which had extensive dealings with several merchants in Barbados.

4

Metallic Currency, 1850–1947

POLICY ON THE ISSUE AND WITHDRAWAL OF BRITISH COINS

The Treasury, in June 1871, announced regulations for the supply of new British silver coinage (florins, shillings, sixpences, and threepences) to the colonies. The regulations were made as a result of representations from some of the Australian colonies to the secretary of state regarding the deteriorated state of the silver coins, and their inability to obtain a new supply from the local banks. Under the regulations, colonial governments were required to pay the Mint the nominal value of the new coin, all expenses connected with its shipment to the colony, including any incidental expenses incurred by the Mint, and also to make their own special arrangements for the supply of coin. With respect to the withdrawal of worn coin from circulation, governments, at their own expense, would send the coin to the Mint, and the imperial government would pay them the nominal value of the worn coin withdrawn from circulation. According to the regulations, applications for new coins should be for the purpose of withdrawing worn silver coins from circulation; bankers and the public were encouraged to exchange old coins for new, rather than applying only for the new coins.[1]

The Colonial Bank, which had always made its own arrangements for the supply of coins either from the Mint or from other banks in England, applied to the Mint in December 1871 for £10,000 in British silver coin for use in the West Indies, but because of the demand in England for silver coin, the Mint could not comply with the request. The Colonial Bank and governments were informed that future applications for coin should come only from governments.[2] The governor of Barbados doubted whether the legislature or West Indian governments had the ability to undertake the new arrangements satisfactorily and indicated the difficulties and inconvenience that would be caused if governments were to assume this function. He proposed that the Colonial Bank in London should stand as the agent for the government. At that time, gold coins were not in general circulation in Barbados.[3] The legislature subsequently passed a resolution appointing the Colonial Bank the agent for the island, with the bank assuming all expenses in connection with the importation of the coin and the return of worn coin.[4]

A revised regulation issued in 1879 specified that the Mint would defray all expenses, including insurance, connected with the shipment of new silver and bronze coins (half-crowns, shillings, sixpences, threepences, pence, half-pence and farthings) to the port in the colony. The colonial government or agent was required to make arrangements for the withdrawal of worn silver coin from circulation and the Mint paid all expenses for its repatriation. The imperial government would pay the government or agent the nominal value of the worn coin withdrawn from circulation. Applications for coin would be made directly to the Mint rather than through the Colonial Office or the Treasury.[5] As a result of the revised regulation, £2,000 sterling in worn silver coin were repatriated in exchange for new silver coin.[6] Some amendments were made to the regulations in 1881, 1904, 1905 and 1909, relating mainly to insurance and the responsibility of the Mint or the imperial government for the payment of returned coin.[7]

Governments in 1920 were given the option to decide whether the Crown's agents should be instructed to ship the new silver coinage on behalf of the government or whether the coins should be issued to the local banks. Barbados decided that the latter method would be the most convenient.[8] Some colonial governments, including that of Jamaica, gave the Crown's agents standing authority to comply with demands for silver from specified banks, but some years later the Government of Jamaica adopted the practice of authorizing each request. The Mint decided not to issue coins to banks doing business in the colonies without covering authority from the government concerned, and relied on the Crown's agents, who were acting as agents for governments, to satisfy it that there was no objection from that government. The Mint also required applications for the redemption of worn or defaced coin to come from an official source.

The Government of Jamaica, in December 1933, enquired whether it was necessary for banks operating in the island to receive its permission to import coin. The Colonial Office decided that, in future, West Indian governments and the banks should ensure that demands could not be met from any source within the colony or from neighbouring colonies before they authorized the export of coins. Governments, on a regular basis, were also required to supply information on existing surpluses to the Crown's agents.[9]

The policy of obtaining coins directly from the Mint was changed in 1934 when the Mint complained of the inconvenience, unnecessary trouble and expense caused by the irregular requisition of coin and short notice given by the colonies for the supply of imperial coinage. Governments and their agents were instructed that the Mint should have specific authority from the government concerned before it would meet the demands for new silver coin; and that the banks in the colonies should ensure, before making a request for new coins, that there were no surpluses in their own branches as well as in other banks.[10]

BRITISH COINS

Branch Mints and Gold Coins

Following the discoveries of gold in Australia in 1851, a branch of the Mint was opened at Sydney, Australia, in 1855, but the coins were legal tender only in specified countries. When the question of establishing other colonial mints was proposed, the Colonial Branch Mint Act 1866 was passed which permitted the Queen to proclaim that the gold coins issued from any branch mint would be legal tender in the United Kingdom and in the colonies. The royal proclamation of 10 November 1866 made these coins minted at the Sydney Branch Mint legal tender in some colonies, including the West Indies and British

Guiana. This proclamation was brought into force in Barbados by the governor's proclamation on 28 January 1867.[11] Subsequently, branch mints were established in other countries in the British Empire.

The royal proclamation of 22 November 1890 declared that, with effect from 28 February 1891, the pre-Victorian gold coins would cease to be legal tender in the United Kingdom and Ireland. An order in council made on 16 March 1892 stated that any gold coins which had not been called in by proclamation and which were below the least current weight provided by the Coinage Act of 1870, if not illegally dealt with, could be exchanged or paid for by the Royal Mint at their nominal value. The order in council was published in the *Official Gazette* on 26 May 1892 but apparently there were no problems in Barbados because a reply was not sent to the secretary of state.[12] Governors were instructed in 1919 to prohibit the export of gold coins but since September 1918, Barbados had prohibited their export except under licence. There were very few gold coins in the island and those were largely used by residents going to Great Britain; consequently, there was no necessity for action by government.[13]

Copper and Bronze Coins

British copper coins were sent to the West Indies in 1817, but they were not well received by the labouring classes. A royal proclamation of 1860 replaced copper coins (pennies, halfpennies, farthings and half farthings) with bronze coins. The copper coins ceased to be legal tender in the United Kingdom in 1869. Governments were asked in 1874 whether they wished to allow the copper coins to remain in circulation or whether they preferred to take advantage of the Treasury's offer to return them to the Mint within a strictly limited period at their nominal value, but after 31 March 1875 (later extended to 31 December 1877) they would only be received by the Mint at the market value of metal.[14] At that time, it was estimated that about £1,500 in copper coins and £500 in bronze coins were in circulation in Barbados.[15] The legislature voted that £125 be used to cover the expenses that would be incurred by the return of the copper coin and also for the inward freight on an equivalent amount in new bronze coins. The Colonial Bank immediately ordered £500 from the Mint and £1,000 at later dates.[16]

Silver Coins

The controversy over the rate of exchange of British silver coins was settled in 1839 but the major problems which remained were the demand and supply of these coins. New coins with the effigy of a new monarch were usually issued after his or her accession to the throne, and changes were made periodically to their designs. Their denominations remained unchanged until 1887 when the double florin was introduced, but the coin proved so unpopular that its coinage was discontinued in 1890.[17]

The coins which generated a great deal of correspondence were the fourpenny pieces called groats, which were in circulation in the West Indies since the 1830s. In 1889, British Guiana made an application for a supply of 120,000 of these coins, and the Colonial Bank also applied for £3,200 for the use of its branches in the West Indies, but by that time these coins were almost extinct in England. The Treasury was reluctant to revive their minting of these coins, although they were still legal tender in England, because they would inevitably find their way back to England where they were considered an inconvenience to circulation. The Mint reported that some of them, which had been sent to British Guiana in the previous year, were already in circulation in England. They decided to issue a special groat with the inscription "British Guiana and West Indies".[18] Governments were consulted about this decision and the governor of Barbados stated that the fourpence coin was very popular, being especially useful in giving change for the $5 and $10 notes issued by the Colonial Bank.[19] British Guiana was assured that when the coins were worn and no longer fit for circulation, and therefore withdrawn, the imperial government would pay the colonial government their full nominal value and also all expenses for their repatriation.[20]

An order in council and proclamation were drafted, but the law officers raised questions concerning the draft proclamation. The Treasury, with the approval of the Colonial Office, decided that

> [I]n those Colonies, in which a power has been reserved to the Queen to legislate by Order in Council, legislation should be effected by such an Order;
>
> That in those Colonies where the power of the Queen to legislate by Order in Council has been expressly parted with or not reserved, legislation should be effected,
>
> (a) as regards coinage either by Proclamation issued under the Coinage Act or by Colonial Ordinance, and

(b) as regards paper currency by Colonial Ordinance.

A legislative Order in Council is the procedure to which recourse may be usually had inasmuch as the power of the Queen to legislate by Order in Council has generally been reserved and has in this Board's opinion been properly reserved; and, if such procedure cannot be adopted, then it appears to My Lords that resort may best be had to Proclamation issued under the Coinage Act 1870 which would accordingly have first to be applied as contemplated under Section 11 (9) in Colonies where it has not already been applied.[21]

Since the queen had not reserved the power to legislate by order in council in the case of Barbados and the Leeward Islands, the Treasury decided that currency matters for these islands should be by the issue of a proclamation under the Coinage Act. However, for British Guiana and the other islands, the queen reserved the power to legislate by order in council.

When the revised draft order in council and proclamations were sent to the office of the Privy Council, the law officer of the Crown, on behalf of the Privy Council, made some amendments to the instruments including making the coin legal tender up to 40s. At the insistence of the Treasury and the Colonial Office, this proviso was deleted because West Indian governments were opposed to a limit on the tender of British silver coins.[22] Proclamations were issued on 9 May 1891 making groats legal tender in Barbados and the Leeward Islands, and orders in council were issued to do the same in British Guiana and the Windward Islands. The proclamation was brought into operation in Barbados on 29 June 1891. Between November 1891 and March 1892, the Mint shipped £2,800 in groats to British Guiana and the other islands, excluding Barbados; however, the Colonial Bank promised to take £800 in 1892.[23] An order in council of 10 December 1901 made groats legal tender in Trinidad where they then circulated freely.

British Guiana in 1915 proposed that it should receive the seignorage on the groat issued to that colony. The secretary of state consulted the other governments concerned regarding the matter.[24] Since the coin then circulated very little in Barbados and its similarity to threepenny pieces caused considerable inconvenience, the governor suggested that the proclamation of 9 May 1891 should be repealed.[25] Replies from the other governments indicated that there was a lack of demand for the coin and had no objection to its demonetization. The Treasury decided that, in lieu of the groat, it would mint a new fourpenny which would be made legal tender only in British Guiana. It also decided that the seignorage should continue to accrue to the British Exchequer. Subsequently, a fourpenny piece was coined by the Mint only for British Guiana and at the colony's expense. Guiana assumed full responsibility for the coin, and the seignorage was credited to the colony. However, the groat remained legal tender in the West Indies and British Guiana but no further groats were minted.[26]

The Legal Tender of British Silver Coins

The House of Assembly in March 1839 passed a bill limiting the tender of British silver coins to 40 shillings but the Council amended the amount to 20 shillings and the House of Assembly agreed. The Council again amended the bill by requiring a suspending clause which the House of Assembly accepted.[27] The act was subsequently repealed because a similar act in Trinidad was disallowed. The legal tender issue was again raised in 1848 when the governor made an enquiry regarding the scarcity of small silver coins. The investigation revealed that there were $18,000 of these coins in the vault of the West India Bank and it was suspected that merchants might also be holding some of these coins since they were too much trouble to count. He proposed to the secretary of state that silver coins under $1 be made legal tender up to £5 sterling, but the Treasury did not believe that the proposal would keep a larger proportion of the smaller coins in circulation or would call for a change in the existing currency regulations in the West Indies.[28]

The limitation of the legal tender of British silver coins in the West Indies was raised by the Treasury in 1852. It was of the opinion that the supply of British silver coin to the West Indies had become excessive for a number of reasons: the Colonial Bank had substituted these coins for silver dollars, which were in demand in Europe; the Colonial Bank no longer found it profitable to procure silver dollars from Mexico; and the British silver coins constituted the reserves upon which its bank notes were based. The Treasury believed that in the event of an unfavourable state of exchanges, British silver coins would not be available for export to foreign countries until the currency of the colonies was depreciated to the extent that there was no difference between its nominal and its intrinsic value. Moreover, a reserve of British silver held as the security for the convertibility of the bank notes in circulation did not afford the same check against overissues as was guaranteed by a reserve of coins of intrinsic value. The Treasury was also of the view that British coins in the colonies should be governed by the same laws as those under which they were issued, and in order to remedy this situation it proposed that an order in council and royal proclamation should be issued declaring British silver coins legal tender for a sum not exceeding 40s. The Treasury also proposed that when a limit was imposed, legal currency should be given to the US gold coins in the West Indies by assigning them a rate that coincided with their intrinsic value and was relative to the standard gold coins of Great Britain.[29]

The Colonial Bank refuted these charges and asserted that its cessation of imports of silver dollars was caused by the war between Mexico and the United States and denied that British silver constituted the reserves for its paper circulation. As proof of this, it indicated that, in the West Indies, while its note circulation in 1851 was £168,215, reserves amounted to £179,453 of which British silver was £98,660. The bank declared that a limited tender would derange the monetary system settled in the West Indies since 1838 (the bank in 1838 objected to the unlimited tender of British silver coins) and would result in a considerable decline in the general rates of exchange. The bank further asserted that limited tender would interfere with existing contracts by increasing debts unless the British government was prepared (1) to take the surplus silver which might be created by the substitution of gold, and (2) also to constantly supply the colonies with gold to replace the coins exported to the United States. The bank indicated that if the proposed measures were put into effect, it would be unable to continue the arrangement of supplying the commissariat with specie at par.[30] The Treasury maintained that its assumptions for limiting the tender for silver were incontrovertible and refuted several of the arguments made by the bank. While the arrangement with the bank for supplying silver to the commissariat was convenient, it refused to allow this convenience to influence its decision on an important question of principle. Since it was responsible for the introduction of the system of unlimited tender of silver in 1838, it was prepared to withdraw a portion of the silver which might be in excess of the requirements of the community for retail purposes when the limit of tender had been established.[31]

The governor was of the opinion that any attempt to change the system would create discontent since there were no complaints either from the local merchants or American traders, and the planters favoured the existing system because it gave them the facility to pay wages in small coins.[32] As replies from the West Indian colonies varied so greatly from each other, the chancellor of the exchequer, Mr Disraeli, concluded that the existence of local laws on the subject and the commercial position of many of the islands precluded a revision of the currency at that time.[33] During 1859, memorials were sent to the secretary of state from some West Indian merchants regarding the rate of exchange between the gold coins of the United States and the sterling, as well as the limitation of the tender of British silver to 40s.[34] After the exchange of several letters between the Colonial Bank and the Treasury regarding the advantages and disadvantages of a limitation, the Earl of Carnarvon was convinced that the question should be decided by the communities whose interests were immediately affected because there appeared to be some anomalies regarding the circulation of these coins in the West Indies which could only be accounted for by local circumstances. However, experience had shown that no inconvenience had been experienced in those colonies in which a limitation had been adopted.[35]

As a result of the demonetization of the silver dollar in the West Indies in 1878, the secretary of state returned to the issue of the defective state of the currency system with a view to placing a limit of 40s to the tender of British silver, and also with the hopes of inducing the mercantile communities to adopt the practice of keeping their accounts in sterling rather than in dollars. He reiterated the disadvantages of the unlimited tender of British silver and submitted specific questions for an enquiry by the governors. The British law officers advised that as the limit of 40s would make all payments beyond that amount not legal tender, the notes of the Colonial Bank would, consequently, not be redeemable in British silver coins beyond 40s.[36] The governor solicited the opinion of interested persons in Barbados and in the other islands under his command (Tobago, Grenada, St Lucia and St Vincent). The views expressed were that

- Sterling was the currency best adapted to the requirements of the islands.
- Although a limit of 40s could be applied to the tender of British silver coin, the proposal was deprecated by the planting and mercantile interests mainly on the ground of inconvenience to internal trade. Other objections were that the present arrangement worked well; that the requirements of the colonies were being met; and that any change would be attended with inconvenience and perhaps with loss. Therefore, it was better to leave things as they were.
- In Barbados it was suggested that if a limit were to be imposed, a notice of six months should be given prior to its imposition.

The governor admitted that the system was defective but stated that any attempt to establish a sound system would cause considerable dissatisfaction. On that account, he did not think it desirable to press for reform at that time. He also stated that since the mercantile community kept their accounts in dollars and cents, a change to sterling was likely to meet considerable opposition.[37]

The Legislative Council of St Lucia in 1888 decided to reform the basis of its currency and to impose a limit on the legal tender of British silver coin. The secretary of state decided that a limit could only be achieved by the concerted action on the part of the leading West Indian colonies and was prepared, as a first step, to extend the limit to £5 or even to a larger amount.[38] The matter was referred to the Barbados legislature. A joint committee of the House of Assembly and the Legislative Council obtained the opinion of merchants, planters and others interested in the question, but the majority of those consulted opposed any change. The committee agreed that it was a sound principle of currency that, in addition to gold being the sole standard of value, there should be a limit to the legal tender of British silver coins. However, it was not unanimous on the question whether, under the circumstances in Barbados, it was desirable to adopt a limit. The reasons advanced were as follows:

- Gold would be unsuitable for the weekly payment of agricultural labourers, which amounted to £7,000 or £8,000, and for the payment of the large numbers of other workers who each received between £1 and 10s a week.
- Frequent importations of sovereigns would be necessary if gold were made the sole legal tender for all large payments.
- The expense of keeping a supply of gold and silver would be greater than keeping only a supply of silver.
- The change would be especially detrimental to the sugar industry, which had bills to sell, although it would be beneficial, to a limited extent, to the merchants who had to purchase bills for remittances.
- If the supply of gold were not always maintained, the rate of exchange would be subject to great and sudden fluctuations which would be prejudicial to the island.

The committee decided that, if a change were made, a period of not less than one year should be allowed to elapse after its legal adoption before the limitation came into operation. A resolution was introduced in the House of Assembly for placing a limit of £5 on the legal tender of silver, but the session ended before a decision was taken and it was not reintroduced at the following session.[39]

A further complication was added when the royal proclamation of 3 February 1898 was extended to Barbados. It declared in part: "In any of the said Colonies or Possessions in which the like coins are at the said date a legal tender for a payment of an unlimited amount, shall continue to be a legal tender for the payment of any amount."[40]

The subject remained dormant until 1900 when an ad hoc interdepartmental committee of the Colonial Office and the Treasury recommended, inter alia, that any colony which decided to establish a government currency note should, in the first instance, limit the legal tender of British silver coins up to £5 and subsequently to 40s. The committee further recommended that the Mint should not bear the cost of freight and other transmission charges of the coins imported into the colonies by the Colonial Bank.[41] The subject was again raised by the Treasury in 1902 in connection with the application of the Union Bank of Halifax to issue notes in Trinidad. In view of the previous opposition from the Colonial Bank and recently from the Bank of Nova Scotia in Jamaica, the Treasury decided that it was not an opportune time to press for this reform because it might tend to discourage banks from developing business in the West Indies.[42]

In the following year the governor of British Guiana was commissioned by the secretary of state to solicit opinions from the other West Indian governments about placing a limit of 40s on the tender of British silver. British Guiana proposed the introduction of a gold coinage and a limitation of silver. The governor of Barbados was of the opinion that it would not be advisable to introduce the measure at that time because of the depressed trade and financial condition of the island.[43] No further action was taken in Barbados on this subject until 1947 when the West Indian governments agreed that the royal proclamation of 14 October 1947, which revoked the proviso in the royal proclamation of 3 February 1898 relating to the unlimited tender of British silver in any colony, should be extended to them. The royal proclamation of 13 November 1947 enabled the legislature of a British possession, where the United Kingdom Coinage Acts were in force, to authorize the issue and use of coins of that possession in addition to those issued by the Mint.

Seignorage

The question of whether the West Indies should receive a share of the seignorage on British silver coins sent to the West Indies was raised on a few occasions. In reply to an enquiry made in 1891 by the Honourable C.S. Farquharson, a member of the Legislative Council of Jamaica, a Colonial Office official observed that it would be difficult to determine the silver coin sent to the West Indies, and that there did not appear to be any very good reason for giving the West Indies a share of the profit. The Treasury stated that the average annual net profit derived from the seignorage on silver coin sent to the West Indies was £3,600 for the years 1872 to 1880 and £19,700 for the years 1881 to 1890. However, it observed that coinage must be treated as a whole and the cost of maintaining the gold coins in a proper condition, in the long run, more than counterbalanced the profit derived from the seignorage on silver. The Treasury's main objection was that seignorage was a right of the imperial government; the profits could not be surrendered as long as the colonies did not contribute proportionately to the expenses of all those functions the government performed for the benefit of the empire as a whole. Such expenses were borne exclusively by the taxpayers of the United Kingdom.[44] However, when the Bank of Nova Scotia in Jamaica in 1899 requested a supply of British silver coins, it was revealed that since 1872 the net issues to the West Indies had been of the nominal value of £1,296,845 and the estimated seignorage was £650,000.[45] In reply to a question asked in the House of Commons in June 1913, the Treasury estimated that a net profit of £200,179 had been made on the sale of British silver coins to the West Indies and British Guiana for the years 1903 to 1912. It is difficult to discover the total value of coins sent to the West Indies and British Guiana because the banks operating in the West Indies received coins from the Mint, the Bank of England and banks in England. For example, the Colonial Bank, in January 1920, stated that in the last ten years it had shipped to the West Indies £905,100 in specie, of which £795,100 had been obtained from the Mint and £110,000 from other banks.[46] There is very little information with respect to coins imported by the Canadian banks. Moreover, there is not much information regarding British coins sent to the West Indies in earlier years. On the basis of the above information, it is reasonable to assume that a substantial profit was made by the Mint on the coins in circulation in the West Indies.

Silver Content of British Silver Coins

In 1919, when the price of silver bullion rose from its pre-war level of about 30d per ounce to 88d per ounce, the British government decided to restore the token character of the silver currency because it was not possible to mint silver coins except at a loss. The Silver Coinage Act of 1920 reduced the fineness of the silver in the coin from 925 fine to 500 fine.[47] In view of the continued high price and the world shortage of silver bullion, the British Coinage Act of 1946 was passed to provide for the gradual introduction of cupro-nickel coinage to replace the existing silver coinage. Certain provisions of the act were extended to the West Indies, British Guiana and some other colonies by the royal proclamation of 14 October 1947. The crown, half-crown, florin, shilling and sixpence made of cupro-nickel were legal tender for a payment of an amount not exceeding 40s, and the threepenny pieces issued in 1937 of mixed metal were legal tender to an amount not exceeding 2s. The royal proclamation was promulgated in Barbados on 26 November 1947.[48]

Surplus of British Silver Coins

During the early months of 1920, banks in the colonies estimated that there was a demand for £100,000 worth of silver coins, but on account of the demand in the United Kingdom for the old silver coin and the inability of the Mint to supply the new coins, the Treasury was unable to authorize their export. Barbados, in May, passed Act No. 20 of 1920 which prohibited the export of bullion, silver coin and bank notes. Towards the end of the year, the Treasury was in a position to supply £50,000, but the majority was not sent to the West Indies; however, the Colonial Office was concerned that the introduction of the new coins might lead to the disappearance of the old coins from circulation.[49] The demand for coins was less acute in those colonies where government notes were in circulation, for example, in Trinidad and British Guiana. The scarcity of coins in Jamaica forced the government in 1920 to bring into force the Currency Note Law which had been passed since 1904.

The problem of surplus coins in Barbados surfaced in 1935 when the government was considering issuing $1 and $2 government currency notes. The banks estimated that their introduction would result in a surplus of £38,000 in silver coin in the island, but the Mint would not normally accept the return of silver coin in good condition.[50] In April 1936, when the Royal Bank of Canada sought permission to export £11,000 in silver coin, which was surplus to its requirements in the West Indies and British Guiana, the Treasury stated that it was not yet possible to receive the whole of the surplus from the colonies. The Treasury noted, however, that it might become feasible over a period of years, provided orderly arrangements could be made for the repatriation of the coins and provided that banks did not export the coin directly to the United Kingdom.[51] Later in the year, the Treasury decided to accept at face value, during its financial year, £100,000 in surplus silver coin from all of the colonies. The term *surplus* was defined as "such silver coin as may be or may become surplus to local requirements if U.K. silver coin remains the local currency, but is subject to the usual legal tender limit of 40s and is not held as part of the backing of the local note issue". It did not cover silver coins that might become surplus as a result of the introduction of a new local coinage. Another condition was that the coin should be received from colonial governments and not from individual banks and that negotiations would be made only with governments.[52]

In the following year, the Treasury decided to accept a further £100,000 in surplus silver. The governor was instructed to enact a Government Currency Notes Bill in order to repatriate any surplus coin resulting from its introduction. In the meantime, the majority of the £38,000 of surplus silver coins had been sent to other islands and, with the imminent introduction of government notes, it was thought desirable to defer the repatriation of any surplus until six months after the notes had been issued.[53] At the end of 1936, it was estimated that the amount of surplus silver coin in Barbados was £9,600; £7,000 were eventually shipped to the United Kingdom in 1938.[54]

By 1942, the problem of surplus coins in the West Indies had been brought largely under control, mainly because of the circulation of government $1 and $2 notes which had reduced the demand for coins. At that time, colonial governments had assumed responsibility for assessing their requirements and for the payment for imports of coin, but the Mint paid the cost of transporting the coin from England to the colonies. However, governments were required to pay for the export of any surplus coin in the absence of special arrangements with the Mint.[55]

FOREIGN COINS

The Treasury in 1852 proposed that when a limitation was imposed on the tender of British silver coins, legal tender should be given to the gold coins of the United States in the West Indies by assigning to them a rate according to their intrinsic value relative to the standard gold coins of the United Kingdom.[56] Although a limitation was not imposed on the tender of British silver coins, the royal proclamation of 19 August 1853 fixed the rates at which these American coins should circulate as a lawful tender in the West Indies. The proclamation came into operation in Barbados on 11 October 1853, and the rates were:

The eagle	41s sterling
The half eagle	20s 6d sterling
The quarter eagle	10s 3d sterling
The gold dollar	4s 1d sterling

The royal proclamation of 9 March 1854, which came into force in Barbados on 11 April 1854, fixed the rates for other US gold coins, that is, the rate for the eagle was applied proportionately to the double eagle and other multiples of the eagle. This proclamation and the 1853 proclamation were extended to British Guiana.[57]

In 1863, American half and quarter dollars began to displace British silver coins in the Bahamas. The circulation of these American coins caused the currency in the colonies to depreciate and the governors were instructed to enforce previous proclamations which regulated the currency of the West Indies. They, therefore, directed their attention to the 1838 proclamation which gave currency only to the Spanish, Mexican and Columbian silver coin. The silver coin of the United States, however, was not mentioned there because, at that time, the currency of those states was based on a gold standard, gold coins being overvalued relative to silver, and the silver dollar being only used for subsidiary purposes. Moreover, the US silver dollar was intrinsically of less value than the Spanish and Mexican dollars and could not be brought into concurrent circulation with them at equal rates. In addition, following the discoveries of gold in California and New South Wales, Australia, a law passed in the United States made the half and quarter dollars a subsidiary coinage, each coin being relatively of less intrinsic value than the whole dollar.

The governor of Barbados gave the assurance that if attempts were made to introduce these coins, the proclamations would be enforced immediately.[58]

As a result of the fall in gold-price of silver, about 1876, the Mexican dollar could be imported into the West Indies for 3s 10d, but the legal rate for this coin was 4s 2d. The governor of British Guiana was permitted to demonetize the coin when a substantial quantity was imported into that colony in May 1876. It was used mainly to pay workers on the sugar plantations. The other governors were directed to report on their circulation and to recommend whether a similar law should be enacted. Since for several years the coin had little or no circulation in Barbados, no action was taken at that time.[59]

The Colonial Bank made representations to the governor in 1878 for these coins to be demonetized. A similar application for demonetization of these coins was also previously made by the Colonial Bank in 1876, but the legislature was dissolved before action could be taken in the Legislative Council.[60] The British law officers in 1878 advised that since the passing of local acts demonetizing the silver dollar, these coins could no longer be legally tendered by the Colonial Bank in redemption of its notes.[61] Although there was no immediate necessity for the demonetization of the coins, the governor was granted permission by the secretary of state to enact such legislation. The Demonetization Act No. 4 of 1879 declared that, in all payments, Spanish, Mexican or Columbian silver coins, called dollars, should cease to be deemed and taken as legal tender. Section 3 of the act stated: "Where in any contract, undertakings or agreement, for the payment of money entered into before the passing of this Act, any sum or amount is expressed in Dollars, the term Dollar shall be deemed and taken to mean the sum of 4s. 2d. British money." People were given three days after the issue of the proclamation to exchange these coins at the Colonial Treasury at the rate of 4s 2d sterling. Act No. 5 of 1893 declared that the Spanish, Mexican and Columbian dollar were no legal tender in Barbados.

The doubloon and its subdivisions continued to be considered legal tender under the royal proclamation of 3 February 1898 when certain provisions of the Coinage Acts were applied with modifications to the West Indies and British Guiana. When the doubloon was demonetized in Trinidad in 1907, the Colonial Bank suggested that it should also be demonetized in the other islands because the bank was obliged to accept the coin as legal tender which resulted in a loss at some of its branches. However, the bank regretted that it had not been consulted before the doubloon's demonetization in Trinidad because the coin was of use and benefit to the community in that colony.[62] In view of Barbados' proximity to Trinidad, the Barbados government agreed that the doubloon should be demonetized as soon as possible.[63] The royal proclamation of 4 June 1908 directed that the doubloon should cease to be legal tender in the West Indies and British Guiana with effect from 1 August 1908.[64]

The governor of Jamaica in 1932 proposed to the secretary of state that the US gold coins and the subdivisions of the doubloon should be demonetized in the West Indies and British Guiana.[65] Action on the proposal was delayed because of its probable effect in those parts of British Guiana where the American gold coin still circulated.[66] The gold and silver coins of the United States and the subdivisions of the doubloon ceased to be legal tender in the West Indies and British Guiana in 31 December 1935 under the royal proclamation of 9 November 1935.[67]

COINS IN CIRCULATION

It is impossible to estimate the actual value of coins in circulation in Barbados during this period. The most reliable information relating to the circulation of British silver coins in the island was provided by the Colonial Bank. It stated that between the years 1866 and 1875, its net imports of British silver coin were £63,050, and that between 1872 and 1890, £10,900 in worn silver coin was withdrawn from circulation.[68] The Mint in 1923 reported that £142,800 in British silver coins and £1,560 in bronze coins had been sent to Barbados between 1910 and 1921.[69]

The Trade Reports from 1900 to 1954 provide data on imports and re-exports of coins, notes and bullion (table 4.1). Between 1955 and 1961, £322,541 ($1,548,197) in coins were repatriated from Barbados to the United Kingdom.[70]

Table 4.1 Imports and Re-exports of Coin, Bullion and Notes (BWI $000)

Year	Imports						Re-exports					
	Total	Silver	Bronze	Gold	Notes	Bullion	Total	Silver	Bronze	Gold	Notes	Bullion
1900	–	–	–	–	–	–	189.1	3.4	–	–	–	185.7
1901	–	–	–	–	–	–	177.4	2.1	–	–	–	175.3
1902	23.8	–	–	–	23.8	–	86.7	7.7	–	–	–	79.0
1903	0.3	–	–	–	0.3	–	44.0	–	–	–	–	44.0
1904	1.7	–	–	1.7	–	–	119.4	–	–	–	–	119.4
1905	2.9	–	–	2.9	–	–	222.5	57.6	–	–	–	164.9
1906	0.3	–	–	0.3	–	–	271.4	–	–	60.6	–	210.8
1907	2.4	–	–	2.4	–	–	149.2	–	–	–	–	149.2
1908	10.2	10.2	–	–	–	–	264.3	1.1	–	65.8	–	197.4
1909	7.1	7.1	–	–	–	–	177.2	–	–	–	–	177.2
1910	4.7	4.7	–	–	–	–	92.3	–	–	–	–	92.3
1911	64.9	64.9	–	–	–	–	69.4	–	–	–	–	69.4
1912	11.2	8.0	1.3	0.3	–	1.6	165.5	0.1	–	–	–	165.4
1913	6.2	5.7	0.5	–	–	–	146.0	30.3	0.2	75.4	–	40.1
1914	1.0	1.0	–	–	–	–	26.4	0.3	–	–	–	26.1
1915	3.4	3.4	–	–	–	–	69.8	0.4	–	51.8	–	17.6
1916	116.7	115.9	0.8	–	–	–	219.1	205.4	0.2	8.3	–	5.2
1917	103.7	103.7	–	–	–	–	25.6	–	–	25.6	–	–
1918	24.3	23.3	1.0	–	–	–	24.0	20.8	0.2	3.0	–	–

Table 4.1 Imports and Re-exports of Coin, Bullion and Notes (BWI $000) *(continued)*

Year	Imports							Re-exports				
	Total	Silver	Bronze	Gold	Notes	Bullion		Total	Silver	Bronze	Gold	Notes	Bullion
1919	184.9	96.5	2.4	–	86.0	–		18.4	0.5	–	1.6	16.3	–
1920	310.4	257.5	–	–	52.9	–		60.3	11.2	–	2.1	47.0	–
1921	16.6	–	1.0	–	15.6	–		194.4	144.0	–	4.8	45.6	–
1922	17.3	17.3	–	–	–	–		198.1	192.0	–	6.1	–	–
1923	37.9	37.9	–	–	–	–		–	–	–	–	–	–
1924	43.2	36.0	7.2	–	–	–		27.1	27.1	–	–	–	–
1925	12.4	11.5	–	–	0.9	–		–	–	–	–	–	–
1926	9.6	9.6	–	–	–	–		5.6	2.8	–	–	2.8	–
1927	105.0	104.7	–	–	0.3	–		1.5	1.0	–	–	0.5	–
1928	54.7	53.9	0.7	–	0.1	–		1.1	1.1	–	–	–	–
1929	3.8	3.3	0.5	–	–	–		29.8	26.4	–	3.4	–	–
1930	24.0	22.6	1.4	–	–	–		7.4	7.2	0.2	–	–	–
1931	12.8	12.8	–	–	–	–		6.1	4.6	0.1	1.4	–	–
1932	67.5	67.2	–	–	0.3	–		8.6	0.6	–	8.0	–	–
1933	102.2	101.3	0.5	–	0.4	–		10.4	4.1	–	6.3	–	–
1934	8.2	5.5	2.4	–	0.3	–		3.9	1.3	–	2.6	–	–
1935	5.9	5.5	–	–	0.4	–		14.4	0.4	3.5	10.5	–	–
1936	1.8	–	1.4	–	0.4	–		35.5	26.2	–	9.3	–	–
1937	6.8	2.4	2.4	–	2.0	–		9.6	0.5	1.3	7.8	–	–

Table 4.1 continues

Table 4.1 Imports and Re-exports of Coin, Bullion and Notes (BWI $000) (continued)

Year	Imports						Re-exports					
	Total	Silver	Bronze	Gold	Notes	Bullion	Total	Silver	Bronze	Gold	Notes	Bullion
1938	79.0	76.7	1.2	–	1.1	–	22.5	21.4	0.1	1.0	–	–
1939	359.9	31.2	3.6	–	325.1	–	3.3	–	–	1.4	1.9	–
1940	45.0	30.2	3.8	–	11.0	–	10.0	–	–	1.0	–	–
1941	78.0	72.0	–	–	6.0	–	25.2	24.0	1.2	–	–	–
1942	90.9	79.2	6.7	–	5.0	–	–	–	–	–	–	–
1943	233.7	205.4	5.8	–	22.5	–	–	–	–	–	–	–
1944	5.4	–	–	0.6	4.8	–	–	–	–	–	–	–
1945	73.4	69.6	3.8	–	–	–	–	–	–	–	–	–
1946	–	–	–	–	–	–	–	–	–	–	–	–
1947	4.8	4.8	–	–	–	–	–	–	–	–	–	–
1948	–	–	–	–	–	–	5.4	5.4	–	–	–	–
1949	36.7	5.8	1.9	–	29.0	–	163.2	163.2	–	–	–	–
1950	9.6	9.6	–	–	–	–	–	–	–	–	–	–
1951	24.6	24.6	–	–	–	–	–	–	–	–	–	–
1952	5.6	5.6	–	–	–	–	–	–	–	–	–	–
1953	1.1	1.1	–	–	–	–	–	–	–	–	–	–
1954	8.9	3.8	5.1	–	–	1.6	–	–	–	–	–	–
Total	2,466.4	1,813.0	55.4	32.3	564.1	1.6	3,392.1	994.2	7.0	357.8	114.1	1,919.0

Source: Barbados *Blue Books* and Trade Reports (various years).

5

The Expansion of Banks and Paper Currency

ON ACCOUNT OF THE failure of the majority of the indigenous banks in the mid 1850s, the Colonial Bank enjoyed a virtual monopoly in the West Indies until towards the end of the nineteenth century. However, this monopoly ended with the establishment of the Canadian banks and with the issue of government notes in the West Indies and British Guiana. This chapter will examine the establishment of the Canadian banks in Barbados; the legislation under which the banks were established and operated; the problems associated with their note issues; the issue of government currency notes; and the restriction on the issue of bank notes.

In principle, the British government was reluctant to make its own notes as well as bank notes legal tender in Barbados. For example, on the outbreak of the First World War, the Colonial Bank and the Royal Bank of Canada made representations to the governor of Barbados to make bank notes legal tender in case it became difficult to import British silver coins and in case the public started hoarding money. The banks admitted that there was no sign of panic on the part of their depositors, but said they proposed the measure purely precautionary. The secretary of state's approval was sought for a bill which had been introduced in the House of Assembly "to empower the Governor-in-Executive Committee to declare Bank Notes to be a legal tender". The Treasury considered the proposed bill inadequate and reluctantly suggested the legislation should follow that of the Jamaica Bank Notes Legal Tender Law. As the problems envisaged by the banks did not materialize, the bill was withdrawn from the Order Paper of the House of Assembly.[1] Another example of the government's reluctance to make bank notes legal tender was seen in 1919. High prices for West Indian commodities and increased wages throughout the area had created a considerable demand for British silver coin, which the Colonial Bank was unable to procure. The bank asked the Colonial Office to permit West Indian governments to issue 50¢ coins, $1 and $2 notes as legal tender, and while these notes were being printed, that British Treasury notes be made legal tender. The suggestion was not accepted by the Colonial Office. Pending the proposed introduction of the Government Currency Notes Bill in 1920, the governor sought approval to make £1 and 10s British Treasury notes (called Bradburys) legal tender in Barbados, but the Treasury and the Colonial Office did not approve the measure.[2] It is to be noted that Jamaica was permitted, during the two world wars, to make bank notes as well as British Treasury notes legal tender. Apart from these occasions, the notes of the Colonial Bank and the Canadian banks in the West Indies and British Guiana were not legal tender and any person could demand specie on presentation of the notes at the respective banks.

In addition to the Colonial Bank, the other note issuing banks operating in the West Indies and British Guiana before 1910 were the West India Bank and the Bank of British Guiana (established in 1837); in Jamaica, the Bank of Jamaica was established in 1836, the Planters' Bank in 1839, the Bank of Nova Scotia in 1889; and in Trinidad, the Union Bank of Halifax was established in 1902 and then acquired by the Royal Bank of Canada in 1910. The issue of notes by these banks created some problems mainly because the Colonial Bank was against this arrangement, as it wanted to maintain its monopoly. The allowance of other banks to issue notes also caused antagonism between the Colonial Office and the Treasury: under the Colonial Bank's charter and according to imperial legislation, the Treasury was responsible for the issue of that bank's notes, while the Colonial governments, subject to the approval of the secretary of state, regulated the issue of notes by the Canadian Banks.

CANADIAN BANKING LEGISLATION

The issue of notes by the Canadian Banks in the West Indies and British Guiana was governed by Canadian legislation as well as by local legislation. The Canadian Bank Act of 1890 provided that the notes issued by a bank should not exceed its paid-up capital. By an amending act of 1899, the limit included any notes issued in colonies outside Canada. According to the Canadian Bank Act of 1913, the notes issued by the Canadian Banks were secured by the following:

1. The amount of current gold coin and of dominion notes held by the banks in the Central Gold Reserves.
2. The Bank Circulation Redemption Fund to which each chartered bank of Canada contributed 5 per cent of its average note circulation, and also a tax of 1 per cent on uncovered circulation which was applied to the redemption of the notes of any defaulting bank. The fund was held by the dominion minister of finance to pay noteholders specie or dominion notes if a bank suspended payment. The payments would be made without regard to the amount contributed to the fund by the defaulting bank.
3. A first charge upon the assets of the bank, including notes issued by the bank in Canada and elsewhere.

The Canadian Bank Act of 1934 consolidated banking legislation.

CANADIAN BANKS

Royal Bank of Canada

The Royal Bank of Canada informed the Colonial Office in December 1910 that it intended to open branches in Barbados and to issue notes not exceeding $200,000 in denominations of $5, $10 and $20. It asked the British government to dispense, either wholly or in part, with the requirement to deposit security against the issue of the notes.[3] Since there was no legislation in force in Barbados to regulate the issue of bank notes, the Colonial Office proposed that legislation similar to that of the Jamaica Bank Notes Law No. 20 of 1904 be enacted.[4]

The Royal Bank of Canada opened a branch in Barbados in February 1911 and the manager, E. Percival, issued the following notice on 8 March: "Interest allowed on special deposits. Drafts bought and sold on Great Britain, Canada and the United States of America. Letter of credit issued and general banking transacted. Savings Department – Deposits of $1 and upwards received and interest allowed at the rate of 3% per annum, added half yearly, at 30 June and 31 December."[5] In March, the bank, with the Colonial Office's approval, issued $50,000 in denominations of $5, $20 and $100. Printed across the face of the notes were the words "Payable at Bridgetown, Barbados".[6] The bank was required to deposit with the Crown agents securities equal to 25 per cent of its notes in circulation, and in October it deposited £15,000 in securities, which were kept by the Crown agents, in a Barbados Bank Notes Reserve Fund. Prior to opening its branch in Barbados, the bank had already established branches in Trinidad and Jamaica.

The Bank Notes Act No. 5 of 1911 provided for the issue of bank notes in Barbados. The main provisions stated that

- a banker should notify the colonial secretary about the amount in value, the denominations and currency of the bank notes to be issued, and the intended date of issue. However, the bank notes issued should not exceed the paid-up capital of the bank;
- a banker should deposit, either wholly or partly with the Crown agents or with trustees in the island, coin or securities approved by the governor equal to not less than the amount in value of the bank notes to be issued or in circulation into a bank note reserve fund;
- the secretary of state could dispense with the requirements with respect to the deposit of securities if he were satisfied that the redemption of the bank notes was sufficiently secured in the Island and in the country of the principal British bank;
- the government had a right to inspect the bank's records in respect of bank notes issued or to be issued or in circulation; and
- the act did not apply to the Colonial Bank.

The act came into operation by proclamation on 15 November 1911.

Canadian Bank of Commerce

The Canadian Bank of Commerce opened branches in Jamaica, Barbados and Trinidad in 1920, and in the following year applied for permission to issue notes in those islands. The Colonial Office was of the opinion that the existing banking institutions in the West Indies were adequate and that further issues of notes might lead to inflation. The Bank of Commerce claimed that one of the note-issuing banks in Barbados had intimated that it did not wish to supply notes frequently to its bank, and if the government did not allow the Canadian Bank of Commerce to issue its own notes, the directors would consider closing its facilities, since the bank would be at a great disadvantage.[7] The Colonial Office was concerned that new banks would insist on having the same rights of note issue as their competitors, and envisaged the time when it might be impossible to grant any more rights to issue notes. The secretary of state instructed West Indian governors to make it known that new banks starting operations in the West Indies should not expect the same rights of note issue as banks which were already in operation. Each case would be considered on its merits, but any bank which might open in anticipation of receiving this privilege should be prepared for a refusal and should therefore ascertain in advance whether this privilege would be granted.[8]

The Canadian Bank of Commerce formally applied to the colonial secretary of Barbados in July 1921 for permission to issue $300,000 in denominations of $5, $20 and $100 under the Bank Notes Act of 1911. The governor supported the application because the bank had given assistance to the agricultural community when other banks had withdrawn credit to the planters, thus enabling several plantations to remain in cultivation and ensuring that Barbadians could find work during a difficult period. The application was also supported by the local branch of the Royal Bank of Canada, which denied the rumour that it was instrumental in exercising its influence by preventing the Canadian Bank of Commerce from obtaining note-issuing powers in the island.[9]

However, in the opinion of the Colonial Office, additional private note issues would complicate the currency, and events in the United Kingdom had led to the suppression of such issues, except by the Bank of England. It suggested that private note issues should be replaced by a government issue or issues. Since there was a proposal to permit both the Colonial Bank and the Royal Bank of Canada to issue £600,000 in the West Indies, it was believed that an issue by a new bank might result in inflation.[10] The Canadian Bank of Commerce had already been granted permission by the secretary of state to issue £100,000 in notes in Jamaica, subject to the condition of depositing 25 per cent of this sum in securities with the Crown agents.

Governor O'Brien strongly supported the application not only because his advisers and the bank had refuted the arguments made by the Colonial Office but also because of the bank's importance to the commercial and agricultural institutions. Moreover, on account of the financial situation of the island, a restriction of credit might have a serious effect. He also pointed out that the issue of government notes would create hardship for the bank and might aggravate the local financial position which was already difficult. The application was also supported by the Colonial Bank and the Royal Bank of Canada, but the latter bank implied that in the event of a further shortage of notes, it might be unable to supply any of its notes to the Canadian Bank of Commerce.[11] The Treasury's view was that the Canadian Bank of Commerce should not be permitted to issue $300,000 worth of notes in Barbados and $750,000 worth in Trinidad unless the governors could give strong reasons why the applications should not be denied.[12] Approval, however, was eventually given for the bank to issue notes in Barbados and Trinidad subject to the deposit of 25 per cent in approved securities to be kept by the Crown Agents.[13]

Colonial Bank/Barclays Bank (DC&O)

The opposition of the Colonial Bank to any competition, which had been directed towards the West India Bank as well as to the local banks in Jamaica and British Guiana, persisted into the twentieth century and was now extended to the newly established Canadian banks in the West Indies, as well as to any institution which offered credit to the planters. For example, the Colonial Bank in 1900 refused to make advances to any planter who had received a loan under the Barbados Agricultural Aids Act, because the latter institution offered lower rates than the bank. The bank also tried to use its political influence to prevent the government from allowing the Bank of Nova Scotia to issue notes in Jamaica in 1900, and in 1905, it bought up practically all the notes issued by the Union Bank of Halifax in Trinidad, thereby forcing that bank to obtain specie for their redemption. One official referred to the Colonial Bank as an obstructive institution and in 1906 Sir M. Ommanney (permanent undersecretary) wrote that "the Colonial Bank, in my long experience, has always shown itself most grasping and unaccommodating and disposed to take the fullest advantage of the monopoly it has so long enjoyed".

Subsequent to the passing of the Colonial Bank Act of 1898, the circulating medium in the colonies (other than silver) was deemed to be insufficient for commerce and trade and great inconvenience was experienced. The Colonial

Bank Act of 1900, authorized that bank to increase its note circulation in the West Indies and British Guiana from £500,000 to £600,000, and the Treasury was given authority to increase, on a temporary basis, the limit on such terms and conditions as might be agreed between itself and the bank.

The Colonial Bank, in February 1908, requested that the Colonial Office amend the conditions which required it to redeem its notes in the West Indies. The bank stated that it was operating at a disadvantage because the charter required it to redeem its notes at any one of its branches other than the branch at which the notes were originally issued, while the Canadian banks, operating under local legislation, redeemed their notes only at the bank of issue; in addition, the public and at least one other bank were using its notes as a form of remittance between the islands.[14] A senior Colonial Office official commented that "the Colonial Bank does not deserve much sympathy. It is ready enough to practice on a newcomer the manoeuvre which it now seeks to guard itself against. But the prosperity of the West Indies is bound up with the Bank. Moreover in most, if not all, of the Colonies it is the only channel of exchange with the U.K. – its rivals are Canadian banks."[15] The background to this issue was that the supplementary charter provided: "That all such Notes be made payable to bearer on demand as well as at such principal Bank or Banks and every of them (if there shall for the time being be more than one such principal Bank) as at the Branch or Agency from which the same shall have been issued." The Treasury explained that when the Colonial Bank Bill of 1898 was being negotiated, a proposal was made that the notes be cashed at par, wherever presented, irrespective of their place of issue. The Colonial Bank at that time pointed out the inconvenience of such a condition and agreed to accept, instead, the designation of a sufficient number of principal banks at which all notes would be payable, namely St Thomas, Jamaica, Demerara, Barbados and Trinidad.[16] The Treasury and the Colonial Office agreed that the application should be declined on the grounds that the public would be inconvenienced by the proposed change and that the remedy seemed to lie in some arrangement with the bank or banks in question.[17]

The Colonial Bank responded by saying that each branch was allotted a maximum issue and the name of the branch was printed on each note and that notes presented in another island in exchange for specie were not reissued in that island but returned to the branch of issue. The bank proposed that it would retain the existing rate for inter-island drafts to induce the public to use drafts rather than the riskier method of remitting bank notes.[18] The Colonial

Office was willing to negotiate on this basis, but the Treasury did not accept the bank's proposal and recommended that the views of governments should be solicited.[19] The governor of Barbados agreed that the Colonial Bank was at a disadvantage compared to the competing banks and it did not seem unreasonable that the bank should be placed on the same footing as its competitors with respect to the redemption of its notes. However, he believed that the withdrawal of this right would be considered by the public as a grievance because, for many years, the public had redeemed on demand the bank's notes at all of its branches and this provided them with an easy method of making remittances without cost. It was also a convenience to travellers and small inter-island traders. The governor suggested that the Colonial Bank should give an assurance that drafts between branches in the islands would continue at the existing rate of one quarter of one per cent, and at a minimum cost of 2½d, and that the notes of bona fide travellers should be payable on demand at all branches, irrespective of their place of issue.[20] Some governments were equally concerned regarding the inconvenience to the public.

The Treasury maintained that the Colonial Bank's proposal was not in the public interest, since the bank still possessed a practical monopoly of the exchange business between some of the commercial centres of the West Indies. However, it was prepared to accept the governments' proposals if they were made a legal obligation.[21] These views were communicated to the Colonial Bank and, in November 1909, the manager met with officials of the Colonial Office to discuss the matter. The meeting was inconclusive because the bank neither accepted the proposals nor offered any satisfactory counterproposals. After the meeting, one of the officials wrote: "Mr. Morrison is the poorest specimen of a Bank Manager that I have ever struck. He understands the routine of his business but he is dull and tedious, with no elasticity of mind, and when he got on to currency he talked amazing nonsense."[22] The Colonial Bank persisted in its demands and, on 25 November, the Colonial Office recommended that the bank seek an interview with the Treasury. However, at that meeting, the bank did not introduce proposals of any importance.

The Colonial Bank, in March 1911, complained to the Colonial Office that the bank's $100 notes issued in Trinidad had been sent by the Royal Bank of Canada in Trinidad to its Barbados branch which was demanding payment in coin for these notes. The Colonial Bank was, therefore, seeking an amendment to the charter that would allow its notes to be paid only at the branch of issue. It requested a meeting with the secretary of state to discuss the matter.[23] The

Colonial Office, however, believed that no useful purpose would be served by granting an interview, and the bank was told to present reasonable concessions to the Treasury.

The Royal Bank of Canada, in December 1911, entered into negotiations to acquire the business of the Colonial Bank and asked for permission to extend its note issue in the West Indies.[24] The acquisition did not take place because of the risk involved in some of the Colonial Bank's accounts in Jamaica.[25] However, the Royal Bank of Canada acquired the Bank of British Guiana in 1914 and was given permission to issue notes up to a maximum of $500,000, encashable only in British Guiana.[26]

The Colonial Bank, in February 1914, raised again the issue of where its notes could be encashed.[27] When it became apparent that the matter of the encashment of its notes could not be resolved, the Colonial Bank, in July 1915, petitioned the secretary of state "to issue to them new and supplementary Letters Patent which while continuing to restrict their note issue as heretofore, will enable them to carry on other banking business without as well as within the limits prescribed in the former Letters Patent but subject to all other restrictions contained therein or in the Statutes hereinbefore mentioned".[28] On 1 October 1915, the Treasury asked the Colonial Bank whether it contemplated the establishment of branches in South America and if so, in what countries. The bank replied that its intention was to open branches in Canada and not in South America.[29]

The Treasury did not agree that the restrictions previously complained of could be removed by the grant of new letters patent, since they were imposed not by charter but by acts of Parliament; consequently, further legislation would be necessary to meet the wishes of the Colonial Bank. It appeared to the Treasury that the real purpose of the bank was to remove the restrictions imposed by the act of 1898, which could be done only by legislation, unless the bank decided to discontinue business under the original charter and the amending acts and reconstitute itself as a registered company under the Companies Acts. The Treasury's policy, since the passage of the Companies Act of 1862 was to oppose granting banking institutions special privileges not allowed under ordinary United Kingdom law or that of a colonial legislature.[30] The Colonial Bank was informed that its power to issue notes would only be granted to a reconstituted company on condition that it agreed not to withdraw any of its existing banking facilities in the West Indies without the consent of the secretary of state.[31] The Colonial Bank decided not to become a registered company because of the inconvenience involved and the possible anxiety it might cause in its note holders in the West Indies. It therefore sought an amendment to its acts.[32]

The Colonial Bank Act of 1916 permitted the bank to establish and carry on the business of a banker in the United Kingdom or in any part of the British Empire. However, the act only allowed the bank to issue notes in the West Indies and British Guiana and did not deal with the question of the encashability of its notes in the West Indies. In March 1917, the Colonial Bank petitioned the Treasury to obtain legislation to increase its share capital and to extend its operations, but the Board of Trade was very critical of the bank's ability, knowledge and facilities to transact worldwide business. However, it was concerned that if the proposals put forward by the bank were not accepted, it might register as a limited liability company under the Companies Acts and withdraw its banking facilities from the West Indies.[33] Notwithstanding these criticisms, the bank was granted permission to obtain the necessary legislation. The Colonial Bank Act of 1917 authorized the bank to establish and carry on the business of a banker in any part of the world where it was lawful for a British subject to carry on such business, with the proviso that the bank could only issue notes in the West Indies and British Guiana. The bank was also permitted to increase its share capital from £2 million to an amount not exceeding £5 million, but it was not allowed during the war and for twelve months thereafter to raise or borrow money without the Treasury's consent.

The Colonial Bank Act of 1925 repealed the original and supplementary charter and all previous acts, and in August, the Colonial Bank received a new constitution. The act increased the share capital to £10 million and authorized the bank to establish "the business of banking in any part of the world in which it may for the time being be lawful for a British subject to carry on such business". Its note issue in the West Indies and British Guiana was limited to £750,000; however, the Treasury could increase the limit on such terms and conditions as agreed to between it and the bank, and the Treasury could call upon the bank to take all reasonable steps to reduce the note issue to £600,000. The Colonial Bank was required to deposit securities with the Crown agents equal to one-third of the notes in circulation up to £600,000 and further security of not less than 100 per cent for the note issue between £600,000 and £750,000, and also to pay interest at a rate calculated to leave the bank no more profit than would cover the expenses of issue. In addition to its permission to issue notes in the West Indies and British Guiana, the bank could issue notes in any other place on the condition that the Treasury and the government concerned agreed to allow the bank to do so. From 15 September 1925 the name of the bank was changed to Barclays (Dominion, Colonial and Overseas).

OTHER BANKS

In 1919, the National City Bank of New York expressed an interest in establishing a branch of its bank in Trinidad. The Colonial Bank drew the secretary of state's attention to the situation in New York where several restrictions were imposed on the operation of foreign banks. After consulting the Treasury, the Foreign Office and the Board of Trade, the secretary of state instructed West Indian governors to take steps to impose on any foreign bank restrictions similar to those imposed on British banks operating in the foreign country concerned.[34] This instruction led to the passing of Act No. 2 of 1920, The Foreign Banks Licensing Act, which provided, inter alia, that (1) no banking business should be carried on in Barbados by any foreign corporation unless it had previously obtained a licence to do so from the governor-in-executive committee, and (2) every licence would be in force for one year and might be renewed annually.

The Bank of Nova Scotia opened a branch in Barbados in August 1956 and in 1969 branches of two American banks were established in the island. These banks performed the usual banking activities but did not issue notes.

EXCESS NOTE ISSUES OF THE BANKS

As mentioned earlier, the Colonial Bank Act of 1900 required the Colonial Bank to deposit approved securities with the Crown agents equal to 25 per cent of its authorized circulation up to a maximum of £600,000. The Treasury routinely granted permission for an increase or reduction of the number of notes the bank issued; however, in 1913 when the bank sought approval for a reduction from £600,000 to £580,000, the Treasury agreed but informed the bank that fluctuations in the market value of its securities were not a sufficient reason for altering the authorized maximum circulation. The bank was warned that should the value of securities again reach £150,000, a subsequent application for a return to £600,000 would not be approved without the production of satisfactory evidence of a demand for an increased note circulation.[35] The Treasury considered note issued above the limit authorized by legislation to be excess note issues.

In 1916, the Colonial Bank was permitted to increase its circulation to the maximum.[36] However, in the following year when it sought an increase of £100,000, the Treasury agreed to the increase for only six months (subsequently extended for a further six months) on condition that interest at the rate of 2½ per cent would be paid on the daily excess issue over £600,000.[37] The excess note issue was extended in 1918 for the period of the war and for six months thereafter.[38] The bank, in June 1919, was granted a further increase of £100,000; however, it remarked that during the war, the Canadian Banks in the West Indies had been permitted to increase their note issue substantially.[39] The bank was apparently referring to the Royal Bank of Canada in Trinidad whose notes in circulation had risen from $400,000 in February 1914 to $1.5 million in March 1915.[40]

When the Colonial Bank was granted a further increase of £100,000 in November 1919, the Treasury raised the interest to 3¼ per cent on that amount and told the bank that if it applied for an extension, the interest of 2½ per cent previously approved on the excess note issues between £600,000 and £800,000 might be increased.[41] The bank contended that the increased interest, in addition to the 3 per cent tax already charged on its note circulation in Jamaica, would result in a loss in that island and probably no profit on the excess issues in the other islands. The Colonial Bank also pointed out that the Royal Bank of Canada was allowed excess issues on which no interest was charged, which placed that bank in a more advantageous position than itself.[42] In Barbados, the Stamp Act No. 3 of 1916 required every bank which was authorized to issue or reissue notes to obtain an annual licence for £75 from the colonial treasurer. The rate of interest was reduced from 3¼ per cent to 3 per cent on the last £100,000, and the Treasury proposed that, in the future, the Royal Bank of Canada should also be charged 3 per cent on excess issues.[43]

As a result of abundant crops in the West Indies accompanied by high prices for commodities, increased wages and the inability of the Colonial Bank to obtain British silver coins, the bank, in December 1919, was granted a further increase of £200,000.[44] Further increases were granted in 1920, which brought the total note circulation of the bank to £1.4 million. The basis for payment of interest on the excess note issues was: first £600,000 free; next £200,000 at 2½ per cent on the daily excess; and the remainder at 3 per cent on the daily excess.[45]

The Royal Bank of Canada in Barbados was also authorized, in April 1919, to increase its note issue by $100,000 entirely in $5 notes,[46] and in January 1920 a further increase of $50,000 in $5 notes in Barbados and $500,000 in Trinidad.[47] At the end of 1919, the Royal Bank of Canada's total authorized issue in the West Indies and British Guiana was $3,405,000, of which $2,454,935 were actually in circulation. The governor of Barbados agreed that the Royal Bank of Canada should also pay 3 per cent interest on its excess issues which would be limited to six months.[48] The bank objected to the payment of interest by any of its branches, especially its Trinidad branch, where the increase of $500,000 was requested by that government, and pointed out that, in addition to the 25 per cent deposit of securities on its circulation in the West Indies, it was obliged to make deposits to the Central Gold Reserve in Canada to the full amount of all excess issues. The bank argued that, on account of these payments, no profit would be made on its note circulation. The bank said that if the Colonial Office insisted on the payment of interest, it would not increase its circulation, which might lead to serious economic conditions in the West Indies.[49] Taking into consideration the currency situation in the West Indies, and the consequence of a shortage in communities of mixed population as in the West Indian colonies, the secretary of state concluded that it was undesirable to risk a shortage of circulation, which would be more serious than that which might be expected from a temporary inflation resulting from an overissue of notes.[50] The excess note issues in Barbados and Trinidad were approved for six months without interest as a temporary measure, and if the currency situation improved, interest at the rate of 3 per cent would be charged on future issues.[51] However, the bank stated that if interest were charged at the end of the six months it would be obliged to withdraw the circulation because it would be operating at a loss.[52] The $50,000 issue in Barbados was extended in June 1921 for a further six months without interest.

Several proposals offered by the Colonial Office, the Treasury and the Royal Bank of Canada were considered with respect to an interest rate to be imposed on that bank in view of the tax which it paid in Canada.[53] After protracted negotiations, it was agreed that the bank would be allowed a total note issue of $2,880,000 (£600,000) for the West Indies and British Guiana on which no interest would be charged and that any excess issues over this amount would be charged interest at such rates as might be fixed from time to time.[54]

At the request of the banks, the governor issued a proclamation on 5 December 1919 prohibiting the export of bank notes except under licence. This measure was taken because large amounts of bank notes had been remitted by the public to the United States and Canada in order to avoid the high rate of exchange charged by the banks for drafts. The secretary of state wanted this restriction terminated as soon as it was safe to do so, but as the Royal Bank was about to print new distinctive West Indian notes to replace those in circulation, the governor suggested that its termination should be delayed for at least six months after the new notes were issued.[55] The Exportation of Money (Prohibition) Act No. 20 of 1920 prohibited the export of silver coin, bullion and bank notes except under licence. The act would be in force until 31 March 1921.

The Royal Bank of Canada, in September 1920, agreed that its new notes issued by any of its branches would be paid at par at any other branch.[56] Later in the year, the Colonial Office advised the Royal Bank of Canada that it proposed to change the currency of bank notes in the West Indies from dollars to pounds. The bank objected on the grounds that the change would mean the replacement of its notes at considerable expense and that such a change would stimulate the agitation for a monetary system based on the US dollar, as had been suggested by the Trinidad Chamber of Commerce. It suggested that there should be a single currency in the West Indies based on dollars and cents.[57] Since the Colonial Office did not think the time was opportune to consider a West Indian issue, the proposal was shelved.

DISTRIBUTION OF INTEREST ON EXCESS NOTE ISSUES

The interest charged on the excess note issues of the Colonial Bank accrued to the British government. In 1920, the Colonial Office and the Treasury agreed that the interest over 1 per cent already received from the excess note issues of the Colonial Bank, as well as the proposed interest on the excess note issues of the Royal Bank of Canada, should be allocated to the West Indian governments.[58] Governments were asked to make suggestions for its distribution, and Barbados proposed that it should be divided, if possible, according to the proportion of the issue notes allotted by the banks to each colony.[59] Following different proposals from other governments, the secretary of state suggested that the interest should be placed in a special fund in England to meet expenditures on matters of general West Indian concern or for minor disbursement, at his discretion (for example, on medical research and the Agricultural College), thereby obviating the need to allocate the interest to particular colonies, which could be very complicated.[60]

In the meantime, the Colonial Bank had reduced its note issue to £600,000 and the Royal Bank of Canada had not exceeded its limit. Since only £8,346 3s 6d had been credited to the fund, the secretary of state suggested that, since the amount was too small to be divided among the governments, the fund could be applied, with their consent, to some purpose common to the interests of those colonies in which the notes of the Colonial Bank circulated. However, he reserved the right to be guided by majority opinion as to the common purpose.[61] Barbados enquired what its share would be before making a decision.[62] When there was no unanimity with respect to the retention of the fund for a common purpose, the secretary of state concluded that the most equitable way would be to divide the fund as follows: one portion in proportion to the 1921 population and the other in proportion to total imports and exports of the colonies for the same year. Barbados agreed to the proposal, but British Guiana did not, having incorrectly calculated that its share would be £4,000.[63] Trinidad proposed that the average note circulation was the most equitable basis for its distribution. The secretary of state finally decided to share the funds based on an average of the gross note circulation in each colony on the last day of each year for the period 1917 to 1921. The governments agreed to this formula. Barbados' share of the interest was 10 per cent.[64]

GOVERNMENT CURRENCY NOTES

In 1900, an ad hoc interdepartmental committee of the Colonial Office and the Treasury recommended the introduction of government currency notes under certain conditions. The auditor general of Barbados suggested that if the recommendations were adopted, government notes should be provided in denominations of 5s and upwards in view of the small amounts paid in weekly wages in the island. He was also of the opinion that a government issue would not drive out the notes of the Colonial Bank, and believed that the notes issued in one colony should be made legal tender in any other colony in which a similar government issue existed. He believed that a small profit might be made by its issue, but the government did not accept the proposal because, at that time, there was not a shortage of bank notes in Barbados, and an issue of government notes might be detrimental not only to the Colonial Bank in its struggle against the existing depression in trade but also to the establishment of new banks in the West Indies.[65] However, in the early 1900s, the governments of Trinidad and British Guiana began to issue government notes, as did Jamaica in 1920. The Leeward and Windward Islands' governments, in later years, also issued notes, but did so for limited amounts and for specific purposes.

When the Royal Bank of Canada in 1911 made a proposal to purchase the assets and assume the liabilities of the Colonial Bank, one of the matters considered by the Colonial Office was whether the opportunity should be taken to introduce a government note issue or issues in the West Indies. However, for several reasons the matter was not raised at that time. The colonial treasurer and the auditor general, while agreeing with these reasons, suggested that government might consider a limited issue of $1 and $2 government notes because the notes would be a convenience both to the banks and to the public by reducing the circulation of silver coins and be the means of easily making the small payments which formed the bulk of business transactions in the island.[66]

The governor in 1913 consulted the banks regarding the issue of government notes. The Royal Bank of Canada was prepared to take £15,000, but the Colonial Bank was unable to commit itself to take a specified quantity before consulting its head office. On the basis of information obtained from Trinidad on the performance of its currency board, the executive committee agreed that an issue should be made and that arrangements might be made with the Trinidad government, whereby its notes could be interchangeable and redeemable at face value with those of Barbados.[67] A draft bill and regulations modelled on the Trinidad ordinance were submitted for the approval of the secretary of state who suggested amendments, especially to those provisions where the term "governor-in-executive committee" was substituted for "secretary of state" as well to make the coin portion of the Note Guarantee Fund 40 per cent instead of 50per cent.[68] However, the executive committee decided not to proceed with the issue on the grounds that it would take years before a profit could be made.

The matter was raised again in November 1920 when the banks experienced difficulty in obtaining silver coins. The planting and mercantile community stated that an issue of government notes of small denominations would be of great convenience to the public and would also alleviate the shortage of currency which then existed. Both banks supported the measure and were willing to take £25,000.[69] The Colonial Office had no objection to the issue of the notes, but proposed that the denominations might be 5s and 10s instead of $1 and $2. When negotiations were taking place with respect to the cost of printing, colour, design and so on, the Colonial Bank obtained £30,000 in silver coins from the Mint. When the coins arrived, there was no immediate need for the issue of government notes and the measure was again postponed.[70] A committee appointed to examine the condition of public finances recommended in 1934 that further consideration be given to their issue since the profits made by the governments of Trinidad and British Guiana on their issues were considerable. It also mentioned that the recommendation made by the 1929 West Indian conference for "the amalgamation of the Government note issues of the various Colonies into a common note issue" was of interest.[71] The three banks operating in Barbados were in favour of a government note issue but pointed out that the measure would result in a surplus of silver coins. The Barbados Chamber of Commerce supported the issue but was opposed to making Trinidad government notes legal tender in Barbados.[72]

A second draft bill was submitted to the secretary of state who objected again to those provisions which departed from the Trinidad ordinance in instances where his approval was required. Notwithstanding the constitutional position of Barbados, he maintained that it was important that any decisions that were to be made about currency matters should be reserved for the British government. His position on the matter had been accepted by other colonies, including Bermuda, where its constitutional position was somewhat similar to that of Barbados. The amendments previously suggested by the secretary of state were incorporated in the Government Currency Notes (Barbados) Act No. 12 of 1937 which was brought into operation by proclamation on 1 April 1938. The act

- called for the establishment of a board of commissioners of currency consisting of the colonial secretary, the colonial treasurer and one other person nominated by the governor. This section was amended by Act No. 16 of 1940 and the composition of the board became two fit and proper persons appointed by the governor. A further amendment was made by Act No. 42 of 1940 to deal with situations where a commissioner was unable to perform his duties;

- defined a currency note as any note issued or reissued by the board of such denomination and design approved by the secretary of state. The notes would be legal tender in Barbados for the payment of any amount;
- called for the establishment of a Note Security Fund, which could be invested in securities guaranteed by the government of any part of the British Empire, except Barbados, or in other securities approved by the secretary of state and held by the Crown agents. A portion of this fund would be held in liquid form, which might be in cash, or on deposit at the Bank of England, or in Treasury bills, or lent out on call or short term, or in readily realizable securities approved by the secretary of state;
- called for the establishment of a Currency Note Income Account into which all dividends, interest or other revenue would be paid, and to which all expenses incurred by the board and the Crown agents would be charged, including a sum equal to 1 per cent of the Note Security Fund;
- stated that at the end of the year any surplus of the Currency Note Income Account should be to be transferred to the general revenue of the island and any deficiency should be met from the same source. However, if the face value of the notes in circulation exceeded the amount of the Note Security Fund, the whole or part of the account would be required to make up the deficiency. On the other hand, if the face value of the fund exceeded 110 per cent of the notes in circulation, the whole or part of the excess should be transferred to the general revenue and the 1 per cent annual appropriation from the account should be wholly or partially discontinued if it appeared to be no longer required;
- indicated that a commission not exceeding 1¾ per cent should be charged for the conversion of currency notes into sterling and vice versa; and
- stated that regulations for the operation of the act required the secretary of state's approval.

The first regulation made on 5 August 1937 provided, inter alia, for the appointment of currency officers, printing of notes, custody of the plates by the Crown agents and so on. It also stipulated that the stock of notes kept by the board should not exceed 500,000 $1 notes and 125,000 $2 notes. A minimum of £5,000 for each transaction was required for the purpose of obtaining notes or sterling from the board or the Crown agents. Government currency notes in denominations of $1 and $2 were put into circulation on 8 April 1938. Although the notes were denominated in dollars, the currency board and the government kept their accounts in pounds, shillings and pence until the passage of the Public Accounts Act No. 1 of 1949 when, with effect from 1 April 1949, a change was made to dollars and cents. All vestries, parochial treasurers, parochial boards and institutions were authorized by Act No. 2 of 1917 to keep their accounts in dollars and cents.

RECIPROCAL LEGAL TENDER OF GOVERNMENTS' CURRENCY NOTES

The secretary of state in August 1940 considered that government notes should be available to meet any demand and should be stored as emergency reserves. He also suggested that, as an additional precaution, the government notes of Trinidad and British Guiana could be made legal tender in Barbados under defence regulations (regulations made during the war) if the reserves in the island proved inadequate, but in advance of an emergency, there would be advantages in doing so by an act. The secretary of state further noted that bank notes could also be made legal tender, but that this should be avoided unless absolutely necessary.[73] Discussions then ensued between the three governors and the secretary of state. British Guiana accepted the proposal that its notes could be used as legal tender in Barbados because it was unlikely to arouse much comment or criticism.[74] However, Trinidad did not agree because the British Guiana $1 note was similar in colour to its $2 note: the concern was that it might cause confusion, diminish the circulation of Trinidad notes and result in a loss of revenue. The Trinidad government, however, decided that, if the occasion arose, its notes should be used in Barbados alongside British Guiana's as legal tender under defence regulations.[75] The governor of Barbados disagreed, preferring instead that it should be done by an act which could be brought into force by a proclamation.[76] The ambivalence of the secretary of state as to which measure – via defence regulations or by an act – should be adopted contributed to the delay.

The matter was eventually settled when a senior Colonial Office official sent a private letter to the governor of Trinidad. He reviewed some of the measures which had been taken in past years as well as recently to achieve a single common currency, and regretted that Trinidad did not see the interchangeability of notes as being desirable. He suggested that the matter should be reconsidered, and concluded that "very much broader considerations are involved than the immediate advantage or disadvantage to the individual territories concerned and it would be unfortunate if the present opportunity of making a little further progress in the rationalisation of West Indian currency were to be missed because of fear of some minor financial disadvantage, which we feel in any case is unlikely to amount to very much".[77] As a result of this intervention, Trinidad agreed to enact the necessary legislation.[78] Barbados passed the Currency Notes (Reciprocal Legal Tender) Act No. 1 of 1941, which came into operation on 1 July 1941 by proclamation dated 25 June 1941. The act provided that, in addition to the Barbados currency notes, the currency notes issued by the governments of Trinidad and Tobago and British Guiana were legal tender in the island for the payment of any amount. Similar legislation was passed in Trinidad and British Guiana. Later in the year, the governor of the Leeward Islands enquired whether Barbados notes could be made legal tender in those islands, and Barbados agreed subject to several conditions. Trinidad government notes were legal tender in the Leeward and Windward Islands but Barbados notes circulated in those islands at a discount.

The construction of US bases in Trinidad during the Second World War created a substantial demand for Trinidad notes. When there was a shortage of notes in 1942, the Trinidad accountant general bought $500,000 worth of $5 notes from the Barbados Currency Board.[79] Except for this transaction, there are no other records of the circulation of Barbados government currency notes in Trinidad and British Guiana. In British Guiana, the banks had been instructed that the government notes of Trinidad and Barbados should not be put back into circulation but should be returned to the territory of issue.

The issue of Barbados government notes is shown in table 5.1. Between 1946 and 1949, their issue remained constant and local bankers believed that this might have been caused by the steady increase of Trinidad notes in circulation in the island. They also speculated that more Trinidad and British Guiana notes circulated in Barbados than Barbados notes circulated in other islands.[80]

There are no records of the actual circulation of the government notes of Trinidad and British Guiana in Barbados. Table 5.2 indicates their notes deposited in the local banks and repatriated to the respective currency authorities, and also the repatriation of notes of other countries.

Table 5.1 Barbados Government Currency Notes Issued

	British West Indian Dollars					
Year	Total*	$1	$2	$5	$20	$100
1938	120,000	80,000	40,000	–	–	–
1939	264,000	171,500	92,500	–	–	–
1940	672,000	497,500	174,500	–	–	–
1941	672,000	499,500	172,500	–	–	–
1942	1,177,000	505,515	156,500	514,985	–	–
1943	1,911,040	433,564	160,356	1,317,120	–	–
1944	2,086,040	372,464	187,256	1,451,320	25,000	50,000
1945	2,086,040	408,264	240,456	1,287,320	75,000	75,000
1946	2,158,040	481,263	317,582	1,151,315	134,980	72,900
1947	2,158,040	528,263	254,582	1,037,315	168,980	168,900
1948	2,158,040	663,263	134,582	1,082,315	136,980	140,900
1949	2,158,040	629,263	60,582	1,088,315	191,980	187,900
1950	2,808,040	680,263	42,582	1,723,315	178,980	182,900

*1938 to 1943 for the year ended 30 September, but 31 December for the other years.
Source: Barbados Official Gazette; Colonial Reports.

Table 5.2 Notes Shipped and on Hand by Banks in Barbados (as at 31 December)

	British West Indian Dollars			
	Trinidad and British Guiana		Other Countries	
Year	Shipped	On Hand	Shipped	On Hand
1946	99,039	18,048	369,864	48,043
1947	207,533	50,904	343,886	44,544
1948	312,667	71,856	399,470	34,963
1949	297,085	122,363	403,710	78,067

Source: Annual Returns on Currency to the Colonial Office

MEASURES TAKEN DURING THE SECOND WORLD WAR

Currency Reserves

The Colonial Office and the Treasury in 1938 became concerned that, in the event of war, there might be difficulties in supplying notes and coin to the colonies. Governments were instructed, in consultation with the banks, to investigate whether there was an adequate stock of currency, especially United Kingdom silver coin, to meet a possible emergency, and that any surplus coin should be retained as an emergency reserve.[81] In anticipation of any problems, Barclays Bank printed additional notes and also sent Bank of England notes to New York which could be supplied to the West Indies in case of an emergency.[82] The investigation by the governor revealed that $168,000 worth of government currency notes were in circulation and $373,000 worth were in stock; the banks had $920,000 in circulation mainly in $5 notes and $360,000 in reserves. The banks explained that the bank notes actually in the hands of the public at any one time was about half of the estimated circulation and that the remainder was in the banks. It was estimated that £84,000 in British silver coins and £2,500 worth of bronze coins were in circulation, of which about 50 per cent was held by the banks as working cash.[83]

The Treasury in 1939, in a letter, permitted Barclays Bank to increase its note issue in the West Indies and British Guiana from £750,000 to £1 million from 1 January for a period of six months on condition that "Approved securities equal to the amount of any excess notes actually issued under the authority of this letter . . . be deposited with the Crown Agents" and with the understanding that the "bank [would] be entitled to retain no more of the profit derived from the excess issue than [would] cover the appropriate expenses of issue".[84] Between 1939 and 1942, Barclays was granted further increases, on the same terms given in 1939, reaching a maximum issue of £1.75 million in December 1942. Thereafter, circulation was gradually reduced to £600,000.[85]

When England declared war, there was a movement of funds from the United Kingdom to the West Indies and the banks became apprehensive about whether the notes available would be sufficient to meet probable demands. As a precaution against possible interruption in communications, Barclays Bank deposited securities with the Crown agents so that local commissioners of currency could issue notes on demand to their banks without further authority from London; £190,000 were earmarked for Barbados.[86] The Barbados commissioners of currency in 1940 had only $457,000 in stock and the governor suggested that $1 million in $1 and $2 notes should be ordered.[87] However, the secretary of state considered that government notes higher than $2 notes should be made available to meet any reasonable demand. An order was therefore placed for $1 million worth of $1, $2 and $5 notes, but the $5 notes were not put into circulation immediately.[88]

In the following year, the secretary of state became increasingly concerned regarding the adequacy of supplies of local currency and directed that the reserves of unissued government notes should be increased to an amount at least equal to 200 per cent of the combined circulation of government and bank notes. In addition, he stated that Bank of England notes should not be repatriated, but held by the commissioners to be used as part of the cover for their note issues.[89] As the total circulation of government and bank notes amounted to $1,369,000 and total reserves $2,879,000, the governor considered that the reserves of the Currency Board were adequate and that to increase them to 200 per cent of total circulation would cost about £2,000 which the colony could not afford.[90] The secretary of state, however, firmly believed that making bank notes legal tender should be avoided and insisted that government notes should be ordered to ensure 200 per cent reserves.[91] As a result, $600,000 worth of $1 and $5 notes were ordered in February 1942 to bring the reserves to 200 per cent, and a regulation was also made on 17 February 1942 authorizing the commissioners of currency to issue their notes against Bank of England notes.[92] Later in the year, a further order for $2 million worth of $1, $2 and $5 notes was placed on account of the high level of bank deposits, delays in printing and shipping notes, and other factors, such as hoarding.[93] The secretary of state recommended that the government should issue $20 notes because the banks should not be the sole source of high denomination notes, and since the US personnel stationed in the West Indies had a preference for high value notes, such notes would be economical to issue.[94] However, there were not a great number of US personnel stationed in the island, so the commissioners of currency did not recommend the issue of the $20 note since the demand might be limited and the cost would be out of proportion to its use. Instead, an order for $2 million worth of $5 government notes was placed.[95]

When the reserves of government notes had reached an acceptable level, the secretary of state designated four islands – Bermuda, the Bahamas, Trinidad and Jamaica – as centres where Bank of England notes would be held, pending repatriation to the United Kingdom. A UK equalization fund was established to pay for these notes submitted to the centres by the commissioners of currency. Barbados sent these notes to the Trinidad centre.[96]

Restriction of Bank Notes

At the same time that the Colonial Office was promoting its wartime policy to increase the circulation of government notes, it was also formulating a policy to reduce the issue of bank notes. The Colonial Office in 1942 proposed that over a period of six months, beginning on 1 January 1943, the note issues of the banks operating in the West Indies should be reduced and stabilized. This involved the reduction of the note issue of Barclays Bank in the West Indies and British Guiana from £1.5 million to the statutory limit of £600,000 (a reduction of 29.4 per cent for the period 1937 to June 1942. In applying this reduction to the Canadian banks, their circulation in the West Indies and British Guiana would be £430,000 or $2,064,000 ($271,000 for the Canadian Bank of Commerce, $500,000 for the Bank of Nova Scotia and $1,293,000 for the Royal Bank of Canada). The banks agreed to the proposed reduction. No legislation was required in respect of Barclays Bank whose excess note issues were authorized on a temporary basis by the Treasury, but legislation was required in the case of the Canadian banks since their circulation was controlled by each government. The proposal was that every month each government would send the value of notes in circulation of each bank to the Colonial Office, which would verify that the global limit of £1,030,000 had not been exceeded.[97]

The Colonial Office also recommended that the commission on the issue and redemption of government notes should be fixed by the commissioners of currency at a rate not higher than absolutely necessary, so that no profit would be made. The commissioners' primary responsibility should be to regulate the exchange rate to ensure that the cost of exchange to the public was kept to a minimum; that is, that the commission should be equivalent to that charged by banks for telegraphic transfers to and from London, and that the same rate should be applied to banks and the public, but that each transaction should not be for less than £5,000.[98] With effect from 1 July 1943, the Currency Board in the various countries of the West Indies charged a uniform rate of commission of $7/16$ per cent for the issue of notes and ½ per cent on redemption, subject to a minimum of £5,000.[99] Previously, they had charged no commission on the issue of government notes.

The Bank Notes (Amendment) Act No. 13 of 1943 permitted the governor-in-executive committee by order to direct any banker not to exceed the value of bank notes in circulation in the prescribed territories, which were defined as Barbados, Trinidad and Tobago, British Guiana, the Leeward and Windward Islands, and Jamaica, including the Turks and Caicos Islands and the Cayman Islands. Similar legislation was enacted in each territory. The Bank Notes Order of 13 May 1943 stated that the limits would come into effect on 1 July 1943.

The Canadian banks were unable to meet the deadline notwithstanding retaining all of their notes received from the public and making all payments in government notes. They suspected that their notes were being hoarded.[100] As the highest government note was for $5, the commissioners ordered $20 and $100 notes to be put into circulation in 1944.[101] On account of these problems, several further orders had to be issued, giving different dates for the coming into effect of the restriction of bank notes. Finally, an order was applied to the Royal Bank of Canada on 1 July 1944 and another to the Canadian Bank of Commerce on 7 April 1945 which brought them in line with the restriction.[102]

The circulation of government notes and the commercial bank notes for the years 1914 to 1949 is shown in table 5.3.

Table 5.3 Notes in Circulation, 1914–1949

	British West Indian Dollars					
Year	Grand Total	Government Currency Notes	Total Banks	Colonial/ Barclays	Royal Bank of Canada	Canadian Bank of Commerce
1914	–	–	n/a		42,840	–
1915	–	–	n/a		60,535	–
1916	–	–	n/a		69,100	–
1917	–	–	n/a		102,880	–
1918	–	–	n/a			–
1919	–	–	462,376			–
1920	–	–	403,083			–
1921	–	–	557,495	310,370	247,125	–
1922	–	–	471,000	263,775	163,915	47,055
1923	–	–	486,041	274,136	144,550	67,355
1924	–	–	468,990	276,970	134,260	57,760
1925	–	–	494,760	281,515	139,995	73,250
1926	–	–	483,285	286,225	117,955	79,105
1927	–	–	510,300	307,240	128,390	74,670
1928	–	–	504,540	309,585	130,700	64,255
1929	–	–	462,605	262,055	122,960	77,590
1930	–	–	428,355	244,205	120,555	63,595
1931	–	–	461,060	264,085	131,510	65,465
1932	–	–	455,415	243,235	156,635	55,545
1933	–	–	507,825	307,055	136,370	64,400
1934	–	–	463,165	281,690	117,935	63,540
1935	–	–	437,475	255,830	111,570	70,075
1936	–	–	458,750	278,450	114,985	65,315

Table 5.3 Notes in Circulation, 1914–1949 (*continued*)

	British West Indian Dollars					
Year	Grand Total	Government Currency Notes	Total Banks	Colonial/ Barclays	Royal Bank of Canada	Canadian Bank of Commerce
1937	–	–	479,720	295,580	108,770	75,370
1938	653,945	168,000	485,945	281,465	118,220	86,260
1939	841,460	264,000	577,460	345,970	136,490	95,000
1940	1,307,435	672,000	635,425	355,425	166,615	113,395
1941	1,391,005	672,000	719,005	414,815	190,640	113,550
1942	2,275,808	1,371,998	903,810	550,595	207,205	146,010
1943	2,221,633	1,911,038	310,595	172,340	85,740	52,515
1944	2,307,980	2,086,042	221,938	122,842	60,442	38,654
1945	2,436,966	2,086,042	350,924	273,461	49,882	27,581
1946	2,530,388	2,158,042	372,346	314,693	39,379	18,274
1947	2,460,456	2,158,042	302,414	258,619	32,299	11,496
1948	2,503,286	2,158,042	345,244	316,646	20,856	7,742
1949	2,572,742	2,158,042	414,700	391,065	16,855	6,780

Note: Notes in circulation for the years 1919 to 1935 are as at 1 December, but 31 December for the other years.

Source: Barbados Archives; Barbados *Blue Books* and Colonial Reports on Barbados (various years).

6

West Indian Currency Unification

BACKGROUND

An ad hoc interdepartmental committee of the Colonial Office and the Treasury appointed to consider the question of the establishment and regulation of the issue of government currency notes in the West Indian colonies submitted its report in March 1900. The committee recommended, inter alia, that if government note issues were established in some or all of these colonies, a foundation would be laid for arrangements whereby the notes issued by any of these governments might be made legal tender in any other colony in which a similar note issue existed, and ultimately throughout the British West Indies. The ultimate goal would be to make the notes issued by the governments current throughout the whole of the British West Indian colonies.[1]

The auditor general of Barbados saw no objection to the proposal, but the governor indicated that the island did not have a shortage of bank notes and was concerned about what effect a government issue might have on the Colonial Bank.[2] As there was little support for the proposal from the other West Indian governments, the Treasury did not recommend its adoption because there would be sufficient bank notes in circulation as a result of the issue by the Bank of Nova Scotia in Jamaica and a proposal from the Union Bank of Halifax to issue notes in Trinidad.[3]

The Colonial Office in 1920 proposed the establishment of a West Indian Currency Board, similar to that of the West African Currency Board, for the regulation of charges for remittances between the West Indies and the United Kingdom, and for the issue of special West Indian silver coins and currency notes which would be legal tender throughout the West Indies. The proposals were not acceptable to the Treasury, in particular the issue of special coins because the withdrawal of approximately £1.5 million worth of British silver coins from the West Indies could not be absorbed in the United Kingdom (it was estimated that £3 million in British silver coin had been sent to the West Indies since 1872) and their withdrawal would cause the Treasury to lose about £700,000.[4]

Following a visit to the West Indies by Mr Wood, the parliamentary undersecretary of state, the secretary of state in April 1922 appointed a committee under the chairmanship of W. Ormsby-Gore, member of Parliament, "to consider what, if any, changes are desirable in the currency systems of the West Indian Colonies, and whether any improvements are required in the existing facilities for exchange between these Colonies and the mother country". The committee reported in June 1923 that the principal obstacles in the way of a combined currency issue by a single authority were as follows:

1. Irredeemable silver coinage [was] legal tender for an unlimited amount.
2. The power of the banks to increase or decrease their issue of notes in the West Indies [had] provided the necessary elasticity in the total amount of currency in circulation, and the facilities open to them in the past to dispose of redundant British silver in London [had] prevented the system from affecting adversely the West Indian exchange with London. But a refusal to take from the banks redundant British silver in London might leave the West Indies on an adverse trade balance without means for correcting the exchanges other than by loans abroad.
3. In all the Colonies, except Jamaica and the Turks and Caicos Islands, legal tender sterling silver circulate[d] side by side in some cases with dollar bank notes and in other cases both with dollar bank notes and with dollar legal tender notes.
4. In all the Colonies except Jamaica the system of currency [was] at variance with the system of money of account.

5. Throughout the Colonies (apart from the Turks and Caicos Islands and from the £1 British Treasury notes in Jamaica) there [were] no units of legal tender in general circulation of higher denominations than 10s. or $2.
6. Government notes [were] legal tender only within the area of the issuing Colony.
7. Government notes [were] convertible only within the Colony and [were] therefore not available for intercolonial or sterling remittances.
8. A substantial portion of the Government guarantee funds [consisted] of token coinage.
9. Any new bank would require new note-issue privileges in order to avoid being obliged to use the notes of its competitors. The Government [would] therefore either [have to] allow the issues to be indefinitely increased or face the possibility that by refusing or limiting the power to issue notes it [would] discourage the establishment of new banks or branches.

The committee recommended the establishment, in the course of time, of a single authority for the issue of currency in the West Indies similar to that of the West African Currency Board.[5] However, the Barbados Chamber of Commerce, the Agricultural Society and the governor's advisers did not consider that any change to the existing system was necessary or desirable.[6] Since the governments of British Guiana and the Windward Islands were the only supporters of the report, the secretary of state decided not to pursue the matter further.[7]

The West Indies Conference in May 1926 endorsed the Ormsby-Gore report and recommended, inter alia, that a specialized conference should be held to discuss the details. That conference was not convened because replies from governments were inconclusive. The secretary of state was of the opinion that a certain amount of misconception existed as to the intentions expressed in the resolution which was passed.[8]

At the meeting of the West Indies Conference in February 1929, the subject of a West Indian currency system was again considered and the following resolution was passed:

> [T]his Conference recommends the continued consideration by the Conference Colonies of the question of the establishment of a West Indian currency system, and suggests the desirability of enquiry as to the possibility of the amalgamation of the Government note issues of the various Colonies into a common note issue, the making legal tender in these Colonies of the Bank of England notes, and the

exploring of the possibilities of the closer association of the West Indian currency with that of the Dominion of Canada; and that the Secretary of State be asked to assist in instituting enquiries on the subject.

The resolution, however, was not acceptable to the secretary of state or the Government of Barbados.[9]

BOARD OF COMMISSIONERS OF CURRENCY, BRITISH CARIBBEAN TERRITORIES (EASTERN GROUP)

The secretary of state in December 1942 revived the idea of a West Indian currency. He reviewed the measures which had been taken since the report of the 1923 West Indian currency committee: for example, the systematic reduction of bank note issues; the reduction of surplus silver coin; the increased circulation of government currency notes which had been brought under the colonial sterling exchange system; the arrangements made between the governments of Barbados, Trinidad and British Guiana by making the notes of each government legal tender in the other; and the adoption of the dollar as the unit of account in Trinidad for government as well as commercial purposes. He suggested that governments should consider taking the necessary further steps for a formal unification and simplification of the currency system.[10] After replies were received from governments, a memorandum entitled "Establishment of a Central Authority to Control West Indian Currency" was submitted to governments for the views of the public and the legislatures.[11] The memorandum summarized the main points in the above despatch as well as those of the 1923 currency committee and outlined the following possible alternatives:

1. The appointment of a Currency Board to control the issue and redemption of notes and coin throughout the Caribbean group of Colonies. This Board would take over existing note issues and issue new notes of its own as and when they were required. No new West Indian coin would be issued until after the war but the Board would assume the responsibility for the supply of United Kingdom coin meanwhile. Notes could be issued in denominations expressed both in B.W.I. dollars and in pounds sterling which would be interchangeable and legal tender throughout the area, passing as £ in Jamaica (and if they participated in the scheme, in Bahamas and Bermuda) and as $ in the Colonies which have adopted the $ as the unit.

2. As in (1), but in issuing separately $ notes in the "dollar" Group and £ notes in the "pound sterling" Colonies. In that event the two kinds of notes could be made legal tender either within their own group only or throughout the area, though no doubt they would not normally circulate outside their own group.
3. The appointment of a Currency Board to control currency of dollar denominations in the Eastern Group of Colonies only.
4. As in (1) or (3) above, but using some other unit in place of the dollar. The West Indian Currency Committee proposed a 4s. 2d. royal and cent scheme, but other alternatives might be preferred: for instance a new unit could be adopted, e.g. a royal or florin of two shillings or the possibility of reinstating the shilling, perhaps divided, as in East Africa, into 100 cents might be considered. If a new unit of say, 2s. were adopted this would be a convenient fraction of a £; notes for less than a £ would then be practicable. This would not involve devaluation; and there might be advantages in ceasing to use the word "dollar" which tends to confusion with the U.S.A. dollar.

The memorandum was published extensively in Barbados and the views of the Barbados Chamber of Commerce and the managers of the banks were especially invited. The opinions on the memorandum may be summarized as follows:

1. There was a preference for establishing a common currency for the whole of the British West Indies, including Bahamas, Bermuda, British Honduras and Jamaica. If the latter colonies were not prepared to come into the scheme, the introduction of a unified currency would be of considerable benefit to the other colonies.
2. The unit of currency should be the West Indian dollar, tied to the pound sterling with a fixed value of 4s 2d. The suggestion for a new unit in place of the dollar was opposed. The Chamber of Commerce was not in favour of notes being issued in denominations expressed both in dollars and sterling.
3. Notes should be issued in denominations of $100, $20, $10, $5, $2, $1 and the coins in denominations of 50¢, 25¢, 10¢, 5¢, 2¢ and 1¢. The commercial banks proposed that the circulation of the new notes should begin as soon as the board was constituted and should not be postponed until the end of the war.

However, the following reply from the House of Assembly was not positive:

The House of Assembly do not know what the possibilities are of obtaining in the West Indies the services of persons with the knowledge requisite to sit on the proposed Currency Board and the likely cost of operating it; they are therefore of the opinion that the formation of such Board should be postponed until after the war when the necessary information should be more readily available.

Subject to the above the House of Assembly are of [the] opinion that notes should be issued separately, i.e., notes based on 4s. 2d. to the dollar in the dollar group and Pound notes in the sterling Colonies and that all such notes should be legal tender throughout the area.

The House entirely oppose the proposals in paragraph 7(4) of the Memorandum (the new unit of account) accompanying His Excellency's Message.[12]

The Seventh Congress of the Associated West Indies Chambers of Commerce which met in Barbados in July 1944 passed a resolution that the time was opportune to consider the introduction of a unified West Indian currency on a decimal system.[13] The governors of Trinidad and the Windward Islands in 1944 suggested that definite proposals for the unification of the West Indian currency systems should be formulated by a committee or meeting to be held under the chairmanship of the comptroller for development and welfare in the West Indies.[14]

In May 1946, a currency conference was held in Barbados under the comptroller's chairmanship. The governments of Barbados, British Guiana, Trinidad and Tobago, and the Leeward and Windward Islands sent representatives, but not the Government of Jamaica, although invited by the chairman. The conference recommended the following:

1. The steps necessary to bring about a unified currency for the Eastern Group should be taken without delay and unification be effected by the establishment of a Regional Currency Board, which should be the sole authority for the control, issue, and redemption of all currency notes and coin in the Eastern Group. The board should be situated in Trinidad and consist of five territorial commissioners appointed by the secretary of state on the nomination of the governors concerned, and a full-time executive officer appointed by the secretary of state;

2. The board should function in accordance with the established principles adopted by colonial currency boards, and the investment of funds in gilt-edged securities should be through the Crown agents in such proportion as the secretary of state might determine;

3. The method to be employed for the distribution of profits between the participating territories should be reviewed, with the approval of the secretary of state, after two years, and after a further three years be subject to review and variation by the board with the approval of the secretary of state;
4. A dollar unit equivalent to 4s 2d in sterling, to be called the British West Indian dollar should be adopted, and the denominations of notes and coins that should be issued;
5. The board should be constituted and begin operations on 1 January 1948;
6. A committee should be appointed to be responsible for taking the necessary steps for the formal establishment of the board.

At the Conference on the Closer Association of the British West Indian Colonies held in Montego Bay, Jamaica in September 1947, governments endorsed the following recommendations of the fiscal sub-committee:

> That the Conference should declare itself in favour of the early establishment of a uniform currency throughout the British Caribbean Territories;
>
> That the Conference should endorse the recommendations of the Report of the Currency Conference held in Barbados in May 1946 suitably amended to permit the participation of Jamaica and British Honduras by increasing the number of Currency Commissioners and to provide for modification of the proportions in which the constituent territories should share in the surplus income or assets, or meet deficiencies, arising from the operations of the Currency Board.
>
> That the Government of Jamaica should be invited to reconsider the position it adopted in relation to the Barbados Currency Conference in the light of the fiscal sub-committee's proposals.
>
> That a Joint Committee Board should be established which should have the sole right of currency issue and redemption in the British Caribbean territories.
>
> That even if at this stage local difficulties prevent the immediate employment of the uniform currency in Jamaica, nevertheless the currency of that Government should be placed under the control of the Joint Currency Board.
>
> That further examination should be devoted to the special case of the currency of British Honduras, to consider the feasibility of bringing it also under the control of the Joint Currency Board. It would be desirable to establish the position of the Joint Currency Board even if this involves separate note issues in the cases of Jamaica and British Honduras.
>
> That as a first step towards informing public opinion of the advantages of a joint currency it would be desirable in the case of the special note issue in Jamaica

to print on the same note values in terms of sterling and in terms of dollars: and similarly the general note issue based on the dollar as the unit of account might also record the equivalent sterling value.[15]

The legislature of Jamaica in March 1948 accepted the recommendations of the Montego Bay conference.

After considerable delay, the governments of the Eastern Caribbean Group accepted the recommendations of the 1946 conference, and the secretary of state's approval was given in October 1947.[16] The preparatory committee appointed to implement the recommendations of the 1946 conference held its first meeting in Trinidad in March 1948 and Mr E.F. McDavid, financial secretary of British Guiana, was elected as chairman. The Honourable H.A. Cuke represented Barbados, and the first executive commissioner was Mr A.P. Dos Santos from Trinidad. Jamaica was invited but did not send a representative. The committee discussed draft legislation based on the Straits Settlement Ordinance of 1938, and decided that its recommendations should be vetted by the legal department of each government and be placed on the agenda for its next meeting. The committee also discussed the repatriation of surplus British silver coin; designs for the notes and coins; office accommodation; staff and other administrative matters.[17]

At the second meeting of the committee, held in Barbados in August 1949, it was agreed that Mr McDavid would continue to act as chairman until its functions were completed and the proposed board of commissioners of currency were constituted. The Honourable Sir Norman Strathie, Jamaica's financial secretary, attended as an observer and stated that there was still the possibility that Jamaica would eventually accept the unified dollar currency of the Eastern Caribbean although it was possible that Jamaica might request that the sterling value should also be indicated on each denomination of the currency notes. The committee agreed that the introduction of notes should be completed before taking action to introduce a new coinage. In light of the suggestions made by the Colonial Office and the legal departments of the islands on the first draft bill, a revised draft bill and agreement were sent to the secretary of state for review and approval. Mr Dos Santos told the committee that he would not accept a renewal of his contract and Mr L. Spence from Trinidad was subsequently appointed.[18]

In September 1949, Mr McDavid held discussions in England with the Colonial Office, the Treasury, the Mint, the Crown agents and the Bank of England.

There, the draft legislation and other matters relating to the Currency Board were finalized. The agreement was sent to the various governments by the secretary of state in November 1949. It provided for the following:

1. The constitution of a board of commissioners of currency to be styled the "Board of Commissioners of Currency, British Caribbean Territories (Eastern Group)" (commonly referred to as BCCB) to provide for and control the supply of currency to the territories administered by the governments participating in the agreement.
2. The sole right of the BCCB to issue currency notes and coins and to assume all the liabilities, obligations and responsibilities of the three existing currency boards.
3. The issue of notes and coins in the following denominations:
   Notes – dollars 1, 2, 5, 10, 20, 100
   Coins – cents ½, 1, 5, 10, 20, 50
   The notes and coins to be denominated in dollars at the rate of 100¢ for each dollar equivalent to 4s 2d sterling in London. The ½¢ and 1¢ pieces were to be made of bronze and the other coins of cupro-nickel.
4. The establishment of a currency fund to be held in London by the Crown agents for meeting the redemption of currency notes. The fund might be invested in sterling securities of or guaranteed by the government of any part of the British Empire (except the participating governments) or other securities selected by the Crown agents and approved by the secretary of state. A portion of the fund was to be held in London in liquid form to be determined by the Board, with the approval of the secretary of state.
5. The establishment of a Currency Fund Income Account into which all dividends, interest and the like would be paid and expenses charged, and 1 per cent of the value of the currency fund was to be paid annually to this fund.
6. The establishment of a Currency Surplus Account (Barbados was entitled to a share of 10 per cent).
7. The settlement by the secretary of state, whose decision would be final and binding on all the governments concerned, of any dispute arising from the interpretation of the agreement.

At the Third Meeting of the Preparatory Committee held in Barbados in April 1950, the revised legislation was finalized and the designs for the currency notes considered.[19] During 1950, the respective legislatures enacted legislation to establish the BCCB. The Barbados Currency Act No. 31 of 1950 –

An Act to implement an agreement to provide for an uniform currency in the Eastern Group of the British Caribbean Territories and for purposes connected therewith – came into operation on 1 August 1951 by proclamation dated 24 July 1951 in so far as it related to currency notes. The act, inter alia, provided that

- the agreement should have the force of law as if enacted in the act;
- the board had the sole right to issue and reissue notes which would be legal tender for the payment of any amount; and coins would be legal tender for $10 in denominations of not less than 20¢, and $2 for lower denominations;
- the Barbados Currency Board should cease to issue or reissue notes;
- the commercial banks, except Barclays Bank, should cease to issue or reissue notes;
- currency notes previously issued by the governments of Barbados, British Guiana and Trinidad would remain legal tender in the island, but no further issues would be permitted;
- currency notes and coins should be converted into sterling and vice versa, and the commission should be charged for the transaction.

After the assent to the above act on 16 August 1950, Barclays Bank granted the Barbados government, with retrospective effect from August 1949, preferential rates on government exchange transactions in London. The government in return gave the bank a reciprocal concession on the rates charged for the issue and redemption of government currency notes. The agreement was criticized by the secretary of state because, inter alia, it established differential rates between the bank and the public who, under certain conditions, had direct access to the commissioners of currency for the transfer of funds. He asked that the matter be reconsidered, but the agreement had already been ratified.[20] The BCCB, at their first meeting, also criticized the agreement made with Barclays Bank. At the meeting, the BCCB confirmed the policy and procedure outlined in the 1950 agreement regarding the operation of the Currency Board as a means of regulating the commission rates charged by banks, and expressed the undesirability of independent concessional arrangements between any bank and any participating government.[21] The agreement with Barclays Bank was terminated with effect from 30 March 1951.[22]

The secretary of state, based on the nominations put forward by the various governments, appointed the following persons as the first commissioners:

Hon. H.A. Cuke Barbados
Hon. E.F. McDavid British Guiana
Hon. A.R.W. Robertson Trinidad and Tobago
Hon. E.A. Thompson Leeward Islands
Hon. L. Cools-Lartigue Windward Islands
Mr. Louis Spence Executive Commissioner

The inaugural meeting of the board was held in Barbados in December 1950 and Mr McDavid was elected chairman. He relinquished that office on 1 July 1951 and was replaced by Mr Robertson.

The BCCB began operations on 28 November 1950, and on 1 August 1951 took over the note circulation of the currency boards of Barbados, British Guiana and Trinidad amounting to $36,438,292 (which included $3,408,040 in Barbados notes) and an equivalent amount in sterling securities from their respective Note Security Funds. Currency notes in denominations of $1, $2, $5, $10, $20 and $100 were issued by the BCCB on 15 August 1951 and from that date the issue and reissue of all bank notes ceased. Barclays Bank had voluntarily surrendered all rights under its charter to issue and reissue notes, and the other banks were debarred from issuing and reissuing notes by the legislation enacted in 1950.[23] As a concession to Barclays Bank, the BCCB in 1952 agreed to waive commission on currency notes issued to that bank for sterling in London to the value of their notes actually withdrawn from circulation from 15 August 1951. The bank's total note circulation on that date in BCCB territories was $1,587,835.[24]

In May 1951, Mr McDavid met with government's financial officials and the managers of the commercial banks in Jamaica to discuss the possibility of Jamaica becoming a member of the board.[25] In December, he held further discussions with the financial secretary of Jamaica and it was agreed that the Jamaica legislature would be asked to approve, in principle, Jamaica's entry to the board and to bring the full scheme into effect from 1 October 1953.[26] At the BCCB's meeting in December 1951, it was suggested that perhaps a more practical proposition might be that Jamaica should merely agree to reciprocal legal tender status for its currency notes as well as those of the Eastern Group whether or not it adopted the proposed common design of the currency notes.[27] Lengthy correspondence then ensued between McDavid, the Colonial Office and the financial secretary of Jamaica regarding Jamaica's participation.[28] In February 1954, Mr N. Holtz, the accountant general and deputy chairman of the Jamaica Currency Board, held discussions in Trinidad with the board's executive commissioner, and an agreement was made on the steps necessary for Jamaica's full participation. The agreement was subsequently ratified by the board in June 1954.[29] Jamaica did not become a member of the BCCB, but the governments agreed that legislation should be enacted in Jamaica and in the other islands to make Jamaican currency notes legal tender in the BCCB territories, and BCCB currency notes legal tender in Jamaica. Act No. 25 of 1955, which came into operation in Barbados on 1 October 1955, made the currency notes issued by the Government of Jamaica legal tender at the rate of £1 for $4.80. Similar legislation was passed in the other territories participating in the agreement and in Jamaica.

Currency notes previously issued by the currency boards of Barbados, British Guiana and Trinidad ceased to be current or legal tender with effect from 2 January 1955 by a proclamation of 15 December 1954. Act No. 19 of 1956 repealed the Government Currency Notes Act 1937 as well as the Currency Notes (Reciprocal Legal Tender) Act 1937. All moneys standing to the credit of the Note Security Fund under the Government Currency Notes Act of 1937 were transferred to the credit of the general revenue of the island, and the Barbados government made arrangements with Barclays Bank for the encashment of its notes still in circulation. BCCB coins were issued on 15 November 1955: the ½¢, 1¢ and 2¢ pieces were made of copper, tin and zinc; the 5¢ piece of copper, nickel and zinc; and the 10¢, 25¢ and 50¢ pieces of copper and nickel. British coins were gradually withdrawn and repatriated.

The Colonial Office in 1954 reviewed the administration of all currency funds, particularly in the statutory requirement that these funds should not be invested in government securities in whose territory the currency circulated. The review indicated that favourable economic conditions derived from the high level of earnings, especially since the post-Korean boom as well as the steady expansion in investment in the private and public sectors, resulted in a large increase in the use of currency in circulation. As a consequence, total currency funds at the end of 1953 in colonial territories stood at approximately £370 million. The review also examined the policy of maintaining 110 per cent cover of the currency funds in sterling investment, and the prohibition of investing the funds of the local government in its own securities. It was concluded that some modification could be safely made without detriment to the stability of the currencies and to public confidence in the fiscal structure of the colonial territories. Since there was a "hard core" of currency which would never be presented for redemption, the British government decided that it would be unwise for any currency authority to hold more than 20 per cent of its currency issue in local securities.[30]

Under the 1950 agreement, the Note Security Fund might be invested in sterling securities of or guaranteed by the government of any part of the British Empire (except the participating governments) or such other securities as, with the approval of the secretary of state, the Crown agents selected. The BCCB, at its meeting in April 1955, accepted the secretary of state's proposals for investing a portion of the fund in locally issued government securities and recommended that not more than 20 per cent of its note circulation should be invested in locally issued securities of the participating governments.

The secretary of state in December 1955 outlined the amendments which should be made to the Currency Acts and suggested that a fixed amount should be written in the law, rather than a percentage, which would fluctuate continuously with the level of currency in circulation. A sum of £2.5 million was suggested, which at that time was approximately equivalent to 20 per cent of the face value of the board's issue at 31 December 1954.[31] The secretary of state approved a draft bill submitted by the governor of Barbados, and Act No. 29 of 1956 was passed to incorporate the proposals.[32] Similar legislation was enacted in the other territories. However, the secretary of state in August 1956 informed governments that he would be unable to give formal assent to amend legislation enabling a portion of currency funds to be invested in local loans unless the territories concerned amended the BCCB agreement.[33] A new agreement, signed on 28 January 1958, replaced the 1950 agreement and was to take effect from 1 July 1956. Act No. 22 of 1959, which came into operation on 1 April 1960, amended and consolidated the law relating to currency and also implemented the agreement. The act incorporated the secretary of state's proposals that the BCCB might issue currency notes to the equivalent market value of securities of or guaranteed by any of the participating governments lodged with the board, and that the Note Security Fund might, with the approval of the secretary of state, be invested in sterling securities of or guaranteed by the government of any part of the queen's dominions, on condition that not more than £2.5 million could be invested in securities of the participating governments, and a portion of that fund was to be held in liquid form in London and could be varied from time to time with his approval.

The Federation of The West Indies was dissolved on 23 May 1962. Trinidad and Tobago became an independent nation on 31 August 1962 and indicated its desire to establish a Central Bank and to issue its own currency. Act No. 45 of 1963, which came into operation on 1 April 1964, provided for the regulation of the business of banking in Barbados. In January 1964, officials of the participating governments and a United Kingdom delegation met in Trinidad to draft a new agreement to replace the existing agreement. This revision was necessary because the Government of British Guiana also wished to establish a central bank and there was no provision in the existing agreement for the withdrawal of any of the participating governments or the consequential action. The officials discussed a draft agreement prepared by the Bank of England as well as a revised version of that agreement prepared by the Trinidad government. The main differences between the two documents had to do with the distribution of the surplus income and assets; the early dissolution of the board and the inclusion of a timetable in the agreement for its dissolution; BCCB coins; and exchange control in British Guiana. At the meeting, it was agreed that the BCCB should cease to issue currency notes and coins in all territories on 1 January 1966; the board should be dissolved on 30 June 1967; and a coin continuation board should be established for a limited period to administer the issue and redemption of the board's coins, the method of distribution of the surplus income and assets of the board, matters relating to exchange control, and the manner in which the agreement should be implemented.[34]

The Government of the United Kingdom (which was responsible for the international relations of Barbados, British Guiana, the Leeward and Windward Islands) and the Government of Trinidad and Tobago signed the new agreement on 12 December 1964. The Trinidad government had insisted that as a sovereign government its international obligations precluded it from signing an agreement with dependent territories. The legal advisers to the British delegation confirmed that Trinidad was right in saying that the agreement must be between the United Kingdom and Trinidad. The preamble of the agreement was as follows:

> Whereas under an Agreement made on the 28th day of January 1958 (hereinafter referred to as "the 1958 Agreement") between the Governments of Barbados, British Guiana, Trinidad and Tobago, the Leeward Islands and the Windward Islands a Board of Commissioners of Currency, British Caribbean Territories (Eastern Group) (hereinafter referred to as "the Board") was constituted to provide for and to control the supply of currency in the territories of the said Governments.

And Whereas Trinidad and Tobago became an independent country on the 31st day of August 1962.

And Whereas the participating Governments and the Government of Trinidad and Tobago:

1. have indicated their intention to establish new currency authorities;
2. desire the Board reconstituted as hereinafter provided to continue to provide for and control the supply of currency in the territories of the participating Governments and in Trinidad and Tobago pending the establishment of such new authorities; and
3. desire to revise the 1958 Agreement and to provide for the Board to cease to issue currency in the territories of the participating Governments and in Trinidad and Tobago on the establishment of such new authorities.

And Whereas the participating Governments have agreed to the arrangements set forth in this Agreement and have agreed to sign this Agreement in token thereof . . . This Agreement shall replace the 1958 Agreement which shall continue to have effect in so far only as is necessary for carrying into effect the provisions of this Agreement.

The Central Bank Act of Trinidad and Tobago came into operation on 11 December 1964 and certain provisions of the act were proclaimed with effect from 12 December 1964. The minister of finance of Trinidad gave a formal "Notice of Replacement" to the BCCB stating that its Central Bank would commence the issue of its notes on 14 December 1964.[35] According to the provisions of that act, the Central Bank was given the exclusive right to issue and redeem currency notes and coin in Trinidad and Tobago, and the Central Bank redeemed $17.1 million of the BCCB currency notes that were in circulation in the island. The sum of $662,494, representing the value of demonetized notes originally issued by the Trinidad Currency Board and still outstanding, was transferred from the BCCB Currency Fund to the Central Bank. Act No. 3 of 1965, which came into operation on 1 June 1965, repealed Act No. 22 of 1959 and implemented the 1964 agreement. The agreement did not come into force until 7 June 1965, mainly because of the failure of British Guiana to enact the necessary legislation; however, Trinidad began to issue notes on 1 January 1965. With the withdrawal of Trinidad in December 1964 and Guyana on 15 November 1965, the BCCB continued to exist but at a reduced level. Under the 1964 agreement, the new commissioners of the BCCB were Trinidad and Tobago, Barbados (which represented the Leeward and Windward Islands, but not Grenada), British Guiana and the executive commissioner. At that time, Grenada was negotiating a union with Trinidad and Tobago and did not become a member of the East Caribbean Currency Authority (discussed below), but used the currency notes of Trinidad and the BCCB coins.

At the end of 1964, $96.5 million worth of BCCB notes were in circulation, and between 1965 and 1967 a significant number of notes were redeemed by the board for sterling by the Central Bank of Trinidad and Tobago, the East Caribbean Currency Authority and the Bank of Guyana. At the end of June 1967, there was only $3.1 million worth of notes in circulation. BCCB coins in circulation on 30 June 1967 amounted to $4.3 million. At the end of 1965, $3.8 million worth of United Kingdom coins which were in circulation in the participating BCCB territories were redeemed and repatriated to the Royal Mint.

The subsequent meetings of the board to wind up its affairs were not always harmonious because of the attitude of the Trinidad representative on the board and some Trinidad officials. The major points of contention were the distribution of the funds in the Currency Surplus Account, because Trinidad had issued notes before the end of the six months Notice of Replacement; setting the date for the demonetization of United Kingdom coins; the representation of Grenada on the board; the establishment of a Coin Continuation Board; the provision in the agreement that certain functions of the board should continue for a period of fifteen years; and the appointment of a new executive commissioner. The final meeting and dissolution of the board was on 14 November 1967. There, a decision was taken to request the Trinidad Central Bank to take over the records of the BCCB from 30 November. The board also decided that, from that date, (1) all balances on the board's books would be transferred to the Crown agents; (2) the Crown agents should be instructed to realize its securities and distribute the proceeds according to the agreement; and (3) the unissued stock of coin should be transferred to the Coin Continuation Board.[36] BCCB notes in circulation in Barbados for the years 1951 to 1963 are shown table 6.1.

Table 6.1 British Caribbean Currency Board Notes in Circulation in Barbados (Year ended 31 December)

			British West Indian Dollars				
Year	Total	$1	$2	$5	$10	$20	$100
1951	3,949,000	620,000	220,000	1,575,000	504,000	630,000	400,000
1952	5,274,100						
1953	5,416,500	803,762	263,762	2,032,540	450,670	1,008,670	858,200
1954	5,477,145						
1955	5,581,624	824,842	139,408	2,118,135	576,260	740,080	1,082,900
1956	5,836,625						
1957	7,261,625	1,011,290	255,733	2,438,667	887,975	1,037,260	1,630,700
1958	6,953,225						
1959	7,629,225	1,147,168	185,637	2,725,665	1,057,395	667,560	1,845,800
1960	7,180,225						
1961	7,019,225						
1962	5,830,225						
1963	6,780,325						

Source: Barbados Colonial Reports

EAST CARIBBEAN CURRENCY AUTHORITY

As a result of the decision of the governments of Trinidad and Tobago and British Guiana to establish Central Banks, the governments of Antigua, Barbados, Dominica, Montserrat, St Kitts, St Lucia and St Vincent decided to establish a common currency, and A.L. Ryan from the Bank of England was appointed in 1964 to make recommendations. Following his report,[37] Barbados passed Act No. 4 of 1965 to implement the East Caribbean Currency Authority (ECCA) Agreement, which was signed on 18 January 1965 by the participating governments, and the agreement came into operation on 26 March 1965. The objectives of the ECCA (the Authority) as defined in the preamble to the agreement were: "to establish a common currency and to establish an authority to issue and manage that currency, to safeguard its international value and to promote monetary stability and a sound financial structure in the territories of the participating Governments". Some of the main provisions of the agreement are stated below.

1. The unit of currency was the EC dollar divided into 100¢ at a parity of 4s 2d sterling.
2. Notes issued by the Authority were legal tender for the payment of any amount.
3. The Authority was to sell/buy sterling for immediate delivery in London at fixed rates.
4. The Authority was to maintain a reserve of external assets for an amount not less than 70 per cent of the value of its notes and coins in circulation and other demand liabilities, but could be reduced to 60 per cent with the approval of the participating governments.
5. A General Reserve Fund should be established.
6. The Authority could purchase and sell treasury bills issued by any of the participating governments, but the holding of these bills of any government should not exceed 10 per cent of the estimated current revenue of that government for its current financial year.
7. The Authority could purchase and sell other government securities maturing in not more than seventeen years, but the holding of these securities at any one time should not exceed EC$3 million or 15 per cent of its notes and coins in circulation and other demand liabilities, whichever was greater.

8. The Authority was empowered to take over the outstanding liabilities for BCCB coin, and the coin taken over was deemed to be issued by the Authority, and it was to act as the agent of the participating governments for implementing their obligations under the BCCB agreement of 1964.
9. Notes issued by the BCCB would continue to be legal tender until a date to be determined by the two authorities.

The Authority consisted of four directors appointed by the Regional Council of Ministers, one nominated by the Government of Barbados, one by the governments of the Leeward Islands, one by the governments of the Windward Islands (except Grenada) and the managing director of the Authority. The first managing director was Mr D.W. Spiers from the Bank of England. The Authority established its headquarters in Barbados on 6 October 1965 and issued Eastern Caribbean (EC) notes in denominations of $1, $5, $20 and $100.

During 1965, the Crown agents transferred the equivalent of $62,188 in sterling to the Authority. This represented the outstanding Barbados government currency notes and the Authority became responsible for the redemption of these notes. The BCCB transferred government debentures to the Authority, which amounted to $2,018,050 held as coverage for its currency notes outstanding in ECCA territories. Between 6 October 1965 and 31 December 1967, the Authority redeemed $27.4 million BCCB notes and received value for the notes partly in BCCB's holdings of securities issued by some of the participating governments and the remainder in sterling. BCCB notes ceased to be legal tender on 31 October 1966, but by agreement between the Authority and the commercial banks, the public was permitted to exchange notes at the banks without charge. United Kingdom coins were demonetized on 1 November 1967 (Act No. 52 of 1967 and LN 150 of 4 October 1967). By Act No. 32 of 1968, the half-cent coin issued by BCCB ceased to be legal tender.

With respect to coins, the 1964 BCCB agreement provided that, when the majority of its coins in circulation in Trinidad and British Guiana had been redeemed, the Authority would take over the liability for the coins remaining in circulation, together with the corresponding sterling assets. It also stated that the Authority should issue these coins to the ECCA governments and Grenada. However, if the coins in circulation in Trinidad and British Guiana warranted it, a Coin Continuation Board, comprising the governments of Barbados, Trinidad, British Guiana and the Authority, should be established to be responsible for the redemption of the coins in the two countries. The Coin

Continuation Board was established in Barbados in 1967, and on 1 January 1970 the Authority took over its assets and liabilities. The board was dissolved on 30 June 1970 and $4.6 million were transferred to the Authority; its surplus profits for the years 1967 to 1970 were distributed to the participating governments of the BCCB.

Barbados became an independent nation on 30 November 1966, but the prime minister announced that his government intended to adhere to the agreement at least until November 1969.

When the union between Grenada and Trinidad did not materialize, Grenada applied for membership to the Authority. The West Indies (Associated States) Council of Ministers and the Government of Barbados in November 1967 appointed a committee of financial secretaries to liaise with the Authority to agree on the terms of Grenada's accession to the agreement. The committee reported in May 1968 on the terms, such as the nomination of a director for Grenada; the share of profits; Grenada's contribution to the general reserve, and the amendments required to give effect to an agreement.[38] In November 1967, the Authority supplied EC$ 1.1 million to the banks in Grenada. Act No. 47 of 1968 provided for the accession of Grenada to the agreement with effect from 17 July 1968.

The United Kingdom devalued its sterling in November 1967 and since the EC dollar was linked to the sterling, the Authority had to devalue its currency to maintain the parity set out in the agreement. Under a sterling agreement made in 1968 between the United Kingdom and the Authority, the Authority undertook to maintain 100 per cent of its external assets in sterling for a period of three years in exchange for a guarantee by the UK government that, in the event of a devaluation of sterling against the US dollar, the UK government would make a payment in sterling to the Authority to restore the dollar value of 90 per cent of its sterling reserves. The Sterling Area Agreement between the UK government and the Authority was extended for a further two years, from September 1971. Under the extension, the Authority undertook to maintain at least 90 per cent of its external assets in sterling for a period of two years in exchange for a guarantee by the UK government that, in the event of a devaluation of sterling against the US dollar, the UK government would make a payment in sterling to the Authority to restore the dollar value of at least 80 per cent of its sterling reserves.

The prime minister of Barbados on 13 June 1969 informed the other governments participating in the ECCA that the Barbados cabinet had decided that

1. Barbados should establish a Central Bank without delay;
2. [Barbados] should continue to participate in the East Caribbean Currency Authority which will continue to perform for Barbados the functions which it now does as a currency issuing authority;
3. This participation should be conditional on the other member Governments agreeing to an amendment to Article 9 of the East Caribbean Currency Agreement in order to enable an independent decision to be taken by the Directors of the Authority in the event of a devaluation of the pound sterling.

On 28 November 1969, the chairman of the Council of Ministers replied, inter alia: "Council is firmly of the opinion that central banking facilities for the signatories to the Agreement would reduce the risk of currency speculation in the area and greatly enhance the prospect for currency integration in the Caribbean. The question of amending the Agreement in accordance with your suggestion is being referred to an expert committee for advice."

The Government of Barbados did not consider that a multinational Central Bank was a feasible proposition, particularly because the decision-making process would not be sufficiently flexible to enable rapid decisions to be made in the case of an emergency. It therefore sought the advice of an expert from the Bank of England on the implications of the establishment of a Central Bank of Barbados while maintaining the association with the Authority in respect of the issue of currency, and also to advise on the possible association of Barbados with the International Monetary Fund. After considering the expert's report, the government concluded that if the Central Bank of Barbados were to be a viable institution and to make a valuable contribution to the island's economic growth, then the Central Bank must exercise, independently, the powers of currency issue.[39]

In 1971, the West Indies (Associated States) Council of Ministers decided to site the headquarters of the Authority in St Kitts. After about two years of intermittent discussions between the Government of Barbados and the other participating governments on the terms of Barbados' withdrawal from the ECCA, a supplementary agreement was finally signed in December 1973. On 31 March 1974, Barbados ceased to be a member of the Authority. Under the supplementary agreement, the Barbados government would receive (1) a share of the Authority's profits as at 30 November 1973 based on the 1965 agreement and also a share of the profits as at 31 March 1974 based on the number of EC notes and coins remaining in circulation in Barbados during the period 3 December 1973 to 31 March 1974; (2) an amount from the Authority's General Reserve

Fund equivalent to 10 per cent of the total amount of EC notes and coins withdrawn from Barbados during the period 3 December 1973 to 31 March 1974 or 43 per cent of the fund, whichever was less. The Government of Barbados would pay EC$350,000 towards the cost of the removal of the Authority's headquarters from Barbados to St Kitts. The Agreement also provided for the redemption of EC notes and coins circulating in Barbados at the parity rate of EC$ 4.80 to £1 sterling.

The Central Bank of Barbados Act No 6 of 1970 came into operation on 2 May 1972, and on 3 December 1973 the Central Bank made its first issue of currency notes in denominations of $1, $5 and $20. On 18 December 1973, $10 and $100 notes were issued. Barbados coins were issued on 4 February 1974. At 31 December 1973, the circulation of Central Bank notes amounted to $28.4 million, and the bank redeemed $22 million worth of EC notes. The legal tender status for the EC notes in Barbados ceased on 28 February 1974 and EC coins on 30 April 1974.[40] The Authority transferred Barbados Treasury bills amounting to $4,321,600 and $3,267,500 in government debentures to the Central Bank in accordance with the agreement. The notes and coins in circulation in Barbados during the period 1951 to 1973 are shown in table 6.2.

Table 6.2 Notes and Coins in Circulation, 1951–1973 (as at 31 December)

	British West Indian Dollars					
Year	Total Notes	BCCB Notes*	Barbados Currency Notes	Commercial Bank Notes	BCCB Coin	BCCB Notes in Active Circulation
1951	5,014	3,949	854	211	–	–
1952	5,649	5,274	274	101	–	3,112
1953	5,671	5,417	183	71	–	3,650
1954	5,673	5,477	145	51	–	3,689
1955	5,694	5,582	81	31	312	4,167
1956	5,936	5,837	74	25	–	4,313
1957	7,356	7,262	70	24	–	514
1958	7,044	6,953	68	23	543	4,979
1959	7,717	7,629	66	22	573	–

Table 6.2 continues

Table 6.2 Notes and Coins in Circulation, 1951–1973 (as at 31 December) *(continued)*

	British West Indian Dollars					
Year	Total Notes	BCCB Notes*	Barbados Currency Notes	Commercial Bank Notes	BCCB Coin	BCCB Notes in Active Circulation
1960	7,268	7,180	66	22	622	–
1961	7,106	7,019	65	22	679	5,033
1962	5,914	5,830	63	21	712	–
1963	6,862	6,780	63	19	813	3,658
1964	5,917	5,835	63	19	854	–

Year	Total Notes	ECCA Notes in Active Circulation	Commercial Bank Notes	Coins
1965	11,285	11,266 +	19	915
1966	14,870	14,851	19	1,046
1967	16,128	16,109	19	1,188
1968	18,159	18,140	19	1,295
1969	20,666	20,647	19	1,527
1970	25,661	25,661	–	1,734
1971	27,938	27,938	–	2,036
1972	31,637	31,637	–	2,226
1973	11,830	11,830	–	2,328

Notes: On 1 August 1951 the BCCB took over $3,408,040 of Barbados government currency notes

*Notes issued

+Includes $62,188 Barbados government currency notes outstanding. The equivalent value in sterling was transferred by the Crown agents to the ECCA in 1965.

Notes in circulation in Barbados include the banks "till money". Net issues to a country do not necessarily represent actual circulation in that country because of inter-island transfers by travellers and others.

Source: Annual Reports of BCCB; East Caribbean Currency Authority and Barbados Official Gazette.

Appendix 1: Imports and Exports

British West Indian Dollars

Year	Imports				Exports			
	Total	UK	USA	Canada	Total	Total Domestic	UK	USA	Canada
1900	5,017	2,142	1,716	374	4,411	3,331	121	2,359	704
1905	5,004	2,135	1,616	401	4,492	3,345	598	1,181	1,322
1910	6,457	2,840	1,918	780	5,226	3,759	563	373	2,607
1915	6,097	2,115	1,918	1,060	5,674	4,035	249	218	3,316
1920	24,699	7,417	8,829	4,951	23,355	17,088	5,066	2,723	7185
1925	11,023	4,007	2,052	2,538	6,821	5,493	984	264	3,933
1930	8,313	2,798	1,636	1,609	5,102	4,020	187	330	3,246
1935	8,836	3,625	1,033	1,457	5,449	4,799	154	445	4,040
1940	11,053	3,967	1,199	n/a	8,073	7,223	n/a	n/a	n/a
1945	16,659	3,089	2,476	7,405	13,777	12,918	5,064	378	6,422
1950	38,726	18,043	2,574	5,589	27,643	25,924	11,334	558	12,266
1955	55,245	22,307	4,176	9,074	38,847	35,779	15,894	804	15,488
1960	83,299	32,748	10,925	8,605	40,912	35,016	24,960	1,082	4,609
1965	116,265	34,446	18,401	14,165	64,269	47,617			
1969	194,554	56,154	43,587	21,531	74,255	57,357	27,268	14,782	2,530
1970	235,005	71,495	49,303	24,635	78,080	61,040	29,873	13,310	2,916
1971	243,685	73,178	44,389	24,974	80,345	53,180	27,106	6,177	3,039
1972	270,436	72,572	51,916	27,116	84,462	63,103	27,775	9,527	4,470
1973	328,602	80,846	69,598	37,260	103,699	83,700	33,455	16,452	5,309

Source: Barbados Blue Books and Trade Reports (various years).

Appendix 2: Exports of Sugar and Molasses

British West Indian Dollars

Year	Sugar				Molasses				% of Domestic Exports
	Total	UK	Canada	USA	Total	UK	Canada	USA	
1900	2,447	83	31	2,311	715	6	670	33	94.9
1905	2,167	432	517	1,144	851	14	805	–	90.2
1910	1,901	324	1,292	217	1,492	48	1,313	127	90.3
1915	2,412	109	2,175	8	1,380	38	1,139	189	94
1920	10,575	4,823	2,210	1,608	6,291	114	4,972	1,106	98.7
1925	3,294	838	2,317	–	1,900	8	1,615	254	94.6
1930	2,271	113	2,094	–	1,467	19	1,149	299	93
1935	1,587	104	1,433	–	3,058	17	2,603	435	96.8
1940	3,111	1,622	1,417	–	3,810	159	3,263	384	95.8
1945	7,626	4,235	3,128	–	3,646	–	3,199	371	87.3
1950	18,567	10,629	7,585	–	5,166	121	4,493	547	91.5
1955	26,525	14,917	11,527	–	4,469	120	3,559	782	86.6
1960	26,833	24,561	2,159	–	3,161	92	1,989	1,051	85.7
1965	33,123	26,082	2,034	–	3,876	72	2,200	1,483	77.7
1969	26,982	26,982	–	–	3,451	22	1,902	1,119	53.1
1970	29,434	29,434	–	–	5,056	15	2,051	2,988	56.5
1971	26,421	26,421	–	–	3,558	16	2,234	1,308	56.4
1972	27,061	27,061	–	–	3,338	16	2,157	779	48.2
1973	32,324	32,305	–	–	4,139	13	1,110	637	43.6

Source: Barbados *Blue Books* and Trade Reports (various years).

Appendix 3: **Banking Regulations**

Regulations and conditions for the observance of which provision should be made in the Charter or Legislative enactments relating to the incorporation of Banking Companies in the Colonies.

Regulations of 1840

[The number in ( ) refers to the 1846 regulations.]

1. The amount of capital of the company to be fixed; and the whole of such fixed amount to be subscribed for within a limited period, not exceeding eighteen months from the date of the Charter of Act of Incorporation. (1)
2. The Bank not to commence business until the whole of the capital is subscribed, and a moiety at least of the subscription paid up. (6)
3. The whole amount of the capital to be paid up within a given time from the date of the Charter or Act of Incorporation, such period, unless under particular circumstances, not to exceed two years. (7)
4. The debts and engagements of the company on promissory notes, or otherwise, not to exceed at any time thrice the amount of the paid-up capital, with the addition of the amount of such deposits as may be made with the company's establishment by individuals in specie or government paper. (13)
5. All promissory notes of the company, whether issued from the principal establishment, or from branch banks, are to bear date at the place of issue, and to be payable on demand in specie at the place of date. (15)
6. No promissory or other notes to be issued for sums under L1 sterling (or in the North American colonies £1 Halifax currency), or the equivalent thereof in any other local currency, and not for fractional parts of that amount. (14)
7. Suspension of specie payments on demand at any of the company's establishments for a given number of days (not in any case exceeding 60) within any one year, either consecutively or at intervals, forfeit the charter. (18)
8. In event of the assets of the company being insufficient to meet its engagements, the shareholders are to be responsible to the extent of twice the

amount of their subscribed shares (that is, for the amount subscribed and paid up, and for an additional amount equal thereto). (17)

9. The company shall not hold shares in its own stock, nor make advances on the security of those shares. (10)

10. The discounts or advances by the company on securities bearing the name of any director or other officer thereof, as drawer, acceptor, or endorser, shall not at any time exceed one- third of the total advances and discounts of the bank. (11)

11. The company shall not advance money on security of lands or houses, or ships, or on pledge of merchandise, nor hold lands or houses, except for the transaction of its business, nor own ships, or be engaged in trade except as dealers in bullion or bills of exchange; but shall confine its transactions to discounting commercial paper and negotiable securities and other legitimate banking business. (9)

12. The dividends to shareholders are to be made out of profits only, and not out of the capital of the company. (12)

13. The company to make up and publish periodical statements of its assets and liabilities (half-yearly or yearly), shewing, under the heads specified in the annexed form, the average of the amount of its notes in circulation and other liabilities at the termination of each week or month during the period to which the statement refers, and the average amount of specie or other assets that were available to meet the same. Copies of these statements are to be submitted to the government of the colony within which the company may be established; and the company to be prepared, if called upon, to verify such statements by the production, as confidential documents, of the weekly or monthly, balance-sheets from which the same are compiled. And also to be prepared, upon requisition from the lords commissioners of her majesty's treasury, to furnish in like manner such further information respecting the state or proceeding of its banking establishments as their lordships may see fit to call for. (19)

14. No bye-law of the company shall be repugnant to the conditions of the Charter or act of incorporation, or to the law of any colony in which the company's establishment may be placed. (4)

15. The charter or act of incorporation may provide for an addition to the capital of the company, within specified limits, with the sanction of the lords commissioners of the treasury; such additional capital, and the shares and

subscription that may constitute the same, being subject in every respect, from and after the date of the above mentioned sanction, to conditions and regulations similar to those applying to the original capital. (20)

16. In all cases in which shares in the company's stock are transferred between the period of the grant of the charter or act of incorporation, and the actual commencing of business of the bank, the responsibility of the original holder of the transferred shares shall continue for six months at least after the date of the transfer. (8)

17. As the insertion in charters or acts of incorporation, of provisions relating to the detailed management of the business of the Corporation, has in several instances been found to render the documents complicated and unintelligible, and has been productive of great inconvenience, it is desirable that such insertion should be avoided, and that the provisions of such charters or acts should be confined, as far as practicable, to the special powers and privileges to be conferred on the company, and the conditions to be observed by the company, and to such general regulations relating to the nomination and powers of the directors, the institution of bye-laws, or other proceedings of the company, as may be necessary with a view to the public convenience and security. (3)

18. Shareholders to be declared a Body Corporate, with common seal and perpetual succession, and any other corporate powers; and with any requisite proviso that judgement against the Corporation shall attach to all additional liability of the Shareholders, as well as the paid-up Capital and other property of the company. (new – 2 in 1846)

18. The Corporate Body thus constituted to be specially empowered, subject to the conditions hereafter mentioned, to carry on for and during a limited term of years (not to exceed twenty-one years unless under particular circumstances), and within the Colony or Colonies specified in the Charter or Act of Incorporation, but not elsewhere, the business of banker; and for and during the like term to issue and circulate within the said Colony or Colonies, but in such manner only as shall not be at variance with any general Law of the Colony, Promissory Notes payable in Specie on Demand. (new – 5 in 1846)

19. The total amount of the Promissory Notes payable on demand, issued and in circulation, not at any time to exceed the amount of the Capital Stock of the Company actually paid up. (new – 16 in 1846)

Form of Return Referred to in Regulation No. 13.

Return of the Average Amount of Liabilities and Assets of the Bank of . . . the period from (1 January) to (30 June) 184.

Promissory Notes in circulation not bearing interest	Coin and Bullion
Bills of Exchange in circulation not bearing interest	Landed or other property of the Corporation
Bills and Notes in circulation bearing interest	Government Securities
Balances due to other banks	Promissory Notes and Bills of other banks
Cash deposits not bearing interest	Balances due from other banks
Cash deposits bearing interest	Notes and Bills discounted, or other debts due to the Corporation not included under the foregoing heads
Total Average Liabilities	Total Average Assets

Notes

ABBREVIATIONS

BA	Barbados Archives
BT	Board of Trade
CO	Colonial Office
CSP	Calendar of State Papers
DO	Dominion Office
FCO	Foreign and Commonwealth Office
HMSO	Her (or His) Majesty's Stationery Office
JCTP	Journals of the Commissioners of Trade and Plantations
SI	Statutory Instruments
T	Treasury

CHAPTER 1

1. No. 83 of 7 May 1661 and no. 84 of May 1661, CSP 1661–68.
2. No. 413 of 11 February 1663, CSP 1661–68.
3. CO 30/3.
4. Ibid.
5. No. 85 of 11 May 1661, CSP 1661–68.
6. No. 1565 of 5 September 1667, no. 1682 of January 1668, no. 1816 of 3 August 1668, CSP 1661–68; no. 341 of 17 November 1670, no. 1116 of 3 July 1673, CSP 1669–74.
7. 23 June 1704, JCTP.
8. James Pennington, *The Currency of the Colonies* (London, 1848), 26–27.
9. No. 74 of 19 May 1720, CSP 1720–21; no. 186(i) of 11 August 1720, CSP 1720–21.

10. 22 August 1724, CO 28/18.
11. 5 July 1739, JCTP.
12. No. 456 of 9 November 1739, CSP 1739.
13. 5 August 1740, CSP 1740.
14. Council Minutes, 17 November 1789, CO 28/62.
15. Meeting of the General Assembly, 18 May 1790, CO 28/63.
16. Council Minutes, 15 and 20 March 1791, CO 28/63.
17. Council Minutes, 20 March 1791, CO 28/63.
18. Moore's Laws, no. 43, 275–80.
19. Council Minutes, 8 June 1791, CO 28/63.
20. Council Minutes, 21 June 1791, CO 28/63.
21. Meeting of the General Assembly, 28 June 1791, CO 28/64.
22. Council Minutes, 2 August 1791, CO 28/64.
23. CO 30/16
24. Portland to Ricketts, circular of 26 May 1798, CO 324/103.
25. Portland to Ricketts, circular of 16 August 1798, CO 324/103.
26. Portland to Ricketts, circular of 8 December 1798, CO 324/103.
27. Moore's Laws, no. 58, 369–74.
28. Ricketts to Portland, 12 December 1798, CO 28/65; Meeting of Committee for Trade, 26 February 1799, BT 5/11.

CHAPTER 2

1. Beckwith to Bathurst, 23 May 1812, CO 318/46.
2. Colonial Office to Treasury; Colonial Office to Committee for Trade, 15 July 1812, CO 319/17.
3. Beckwith to Bathurst, 21 June 1813, CO 318/48.
4. Jordan to Committee for Trade, 6 March 1816, BT 6/125.
5. *Barbados Mercury and Colonial Advocate*, 25 March 1817.
6. Bathurst to Combermere, circular of 18 December 1817, CO 29/30.
7. Combermere to Bathurst, no. 25 of 19 March 1818, CO 28/87; *Barbados Mercury and Colonial Gazette*, 6 March 1819.
8. Colonial Office to Island Agents, 17 September 1819, CO 319/23.
9. Bathurst to Warde, circular of 14 March 1822, CO 854/1.
10. *Barbadian*, 15 February 1823.
11. Mint 13/15.
12. Colonial Bank to Treasury, 29 June 1852 and 9 July 1853, T 1/5807A.

13. Treasury to Colonial Bank, 1 July 1853 and 3 August 1853, T 27/120.
14. Bathurst to Warde, circular of 18 May 1825, CO 854/1.
15. Treasury to Colonial Office, 22 April 1825, CO 28/51.
16. Treasury circular dated 12 February 1825, CO 318/133.
17. Deputy Commissary General (DCG) to Treasury, 7 November 1831, T 1/2932.
18. Meeting of Privy Council, 6 September 1825, CO 31/48; *Barbadian*, 9 September 1825.
19. DCG to Treasury, 28 December 1825, T 1/3624.
20. DCG to Treasury, 26 August 1825, T 1/3625.
21. Lord Robert Chalmers, *A History of Currency in the British Colonies* (London, 1893), 25–26.
22. Treasury circular no. 125 dated 21 September 1827, T 1/3619.
23. Treasury circular no. 193 dated 24 June 1835, T 27/98.
24. F.W.N. Bayley, *Four Years' Residence in the West Indies, 1826–1829* (London: William Kidd, 1833), 64–65.
25. DCG to Treasury, 3 January 1834, T 1/3619.
26. Treasury to Mint, 25 January 1834, Mint 1/32.
27. Treasury Minute, 21 February 1834, CO 318/118.
28. Stanley to Smith, circular of 5 April 1834, CO 854/1.
29. Smith to Rice, General no. 10 of 17 August 1834, CO 412/65.
30. Minutes of the General Assembly, 3 June 1834, CO 31/53.
31. Minutes of the General Assembly, 24 June 1834, CO 31/53.
32. Minutes of the General Assembly, 2 July 1834, CO 31/53.
33. Smith to Rice, No 23 of 14 July 1834, CO 28/113.
34. Colonial Office to Treasury, 25 March 1835, CO 319/33.
35. Mint to Treasury, 31 March 1835, T 1/3625.
36. Treasury to Colonial Office, 8 May 1835, CO 318/120; Colonial Office to Secretary of the Committee, 11 May 1835, CO 319/33.
37. DCG to Treasury, 30 June 1835, T 1/3625; Treasury to DCG, 31 August 1835, T 1/3625.
38. 28 October 1835, T 1/4224.
39. Mint to Treasury, 1 March 1836, Mint 1/33; Treasury to Mint, 8 March 1836, Mint 1/33.
40. Treasury to Mint, 2 November 1838, Mint 1/35.
41. Colonial Bank to Treasury, 8 June 1841, T 1/4592; Mint to Treasury, 15 June 1841, T 1/4592; Treasury to Mint, 23 July 1841, Mint 1/37.
42. Mint to Treasury, 7 May 1845 Mint 1/39; Treasury to Mint, 19 May 1845, T 27/131.

43. Mint to Treasury, 27 March 1846 Mint 1/40; Treasury to Mint, 19 May 1845, T 27/131.
44. Minutes of the General Assembly, 26 January 1836, CO 31/53.
45. Smith to Glenelg, no. 24 of 13 April 1836, CO 28/117.
46. Smith to Glenelg, no. 12 of 23 February 1836, CO 28/117.
47. Treasury Minute, 3 February 1836, T 1/3625; DCG to Treasury, 23 May 1836, T 1/3625.
48. Smith to Glenelg, no. 44 of 15 July 1836, CO 28/117.
49. Colonial Office to Treasury, 20 September 1836, CO 29/34; Treasury to Colonial Office, 30 September 1836, CO 28/118.
50. DCG to Treasury, 25 May 1836, T 1/3625.
51. Glenelg to Smith, circular of 31 August 1836, CO 854/1.
52. Meeting of Privy Council, 28 September 1836; *Barbadian*, 1 October 1836.
53. T 1/3624 – *Barbados Globe and Colonial Advocate*, 4 May 1837; *Barbados Mercury*, 2 and 6 May 1837.
54. MacGregor to Glenelg, no. 95 of 8 May 1837, CO 28/119; Colonial Office to Treasury, 26 June 1837, CO 29/34; Treasury to Colonial Office, 1 July 1837, CO 28/121; Glenelg to MacGregor, no. 42 of 14 July 1837, CO 28/119.
55. Meeting of Privy Council, 19 August 1837; *Barbadian*, 23 August 1837.
56. Glenelg to Agents, 1 May 1838, CO 318/132.
57. Agents to Glenelg, 4 and 8 May 1838, CO 318/134.
58. MacGregor to Glenelg, no. 109 of 12 May 1838, CO 28/122; Glenelg to MacGregor, no. 111 of 29 August 1838, CO 28/122.
59. MacGregor to Glenelg, no. 343 of 4 December 1838, CO 29/36.
60. *Barbados Mercury*, 7 September 1838; *Liberal*, 12 September 1838.
61. *Liberal*, 19 September 1838.
62. DCG to Treasury, 15 May 1834, T 1/3625.
63. Pennington, *Currency*, 26–27; H.A. Shannon, Evolution of Colonial Sterling Exchange Standard, IMF Staff Papers, vol. 1 of 1950–1951.
64. Glenelg to MacGregor, circular of 2 July 1838, CO 854/2.
65. Glenelg to MacGregor, 15 August 1838, CO 318/132.
66. Glenelg to MacGregor, circular of 15 September 1838, CO 854/2.
67. *Barbados Mercury*, 27 October 1838.
68. DCG to Treasury, 3 November 1838, T 1/3624.
69. DCG to Treasury, 15 December 1838, T 1/3624.
70. MacGregor to Glenelg, no. 298 of 3 November 1838, CO 28/124.
71. T 1/3624 – *Barbados Globe and Colonial Advocate*, 15 November 1838.
72. MacGregor to Glenelg, no. 343 of 14 December 1838, CO 28/124; Normandy to MacGregor, no. 140 of 13 February 1839, CO 28/132.

73. Normandy to MacGregor, no. 6 of 14 March 1839, CO 28/132.
74. Council Office to Colonial Office, 27 March 1839, CO 28/132.
75. Colonial Office to Council Office, 5 April 1839, CO 28/132; Council Office to Colonial Office, 1 May,1839, CO 28/132; Colonial Office to Treasury, 20 May 1839, CO 28/132.
76. Treasury to Colonial Office, 8 June 1839, CO 28/132; Colonial Office to Council Office, 20 June 1839, CO 28/132.
77. Normandy to MacGregor, no. 31 of 13 July 1839, CO 28/132.
78. DCG to Treasury, 24 April, 1839, T 1/3624.
79. Treasury to Colonial Bank, 29 January 1840, T 27/105; Treasury to Colonial Bank, 20 April 1840, T 27/106.
80. Treasury to Colonial Bank, 28 April 1845, T 27/114.
81. Treasury to Colonial Office, 27 January 1848, CO 28/169.
82. Colonial Office to Treasury, 15 January 1848, CO 28/169; Treasury Minute of 25 January 1848, CO 28/169.
83. *Barbadian*, 1 April 1848.
84. Grey to Stanley, no. 13 of 22 March 1845, CO 28/161.
85. Stanley to Grey, no. 137 of 28 June 1845, CO 28/161; Stanley to Grey, no. 70 of 30 August 1845, CO 28/161.
86. Minutes of the General Assembly, 21 October 1845, CO 31/56.
87. Minutes of the General Assembly, 1 September 1835, CO 31/53.

CHAPTER 3

1. 11 November 1831, T 1/3472.
2. 12 April 1833, T 1/3472.
3. Chalmers, *History of Currency*, 32–33.
4. Treasury to Committee for Trade, 14 June 1853, BT 9/10; Committee for Trade to Treasury, 16 June 1853, BT 3/44.
5. *A Banking Centenary, Barclays Bank (Dominion, Colonial and Overseas), 1836–1936* (London: William Brendon and Sons, 1938); A.S. Baster, *The Imperial Banks* (London, 1929).
6. Colonial Office to Committee for Trade, 18 February 1836, BT 1/317.
7. Mint to Treasury, 15 August 1836, BT 1/327.
8. Committee for Trade to Treasury, 14 December 1836, T 1/3625; Glenelg to MacGregor, circular of 30 December 1836, CO 854/1.
9. Colonial Bank to Treasury, 28 January 1837, T 1/3625.

10. Colonial Bank to Treasury, 28 June 1837, T 1/3625; Treasury to Colonial Bank, 21 July 1837, T 1/3625; Colonial Bank to Treasury, 27 July 1837, T 1/3625.
11. Grey to MacGregor, circulars of 1 November 1836 and 16 January 1837, CO 854/1.
12. *Barbados Mercury*, 6 May 1837.
13. Colonial Bank to Collector of Customs, 19 May 1837, T 1/3624; Collector of Customs to Commissioners of HM Customs, 26 May 1837, T 1/3624; Treasury to Colonial Office, 27 November 1837, CO 28/121.
14. Colonial Bank to Colonial Office, 29 July 1837, CO 318/123; Treasury to Colonial Office, 16 August 1837, CO 318/123; Colonial Office to Colonial Bank, 26 August 1837, CO 319/35.
15. Glenelg to MacGregor, circular of 30 November 1837, CO 854/2.
16. Colonial Bank to Committee for Trade, 19 July 1838, BT 1/342; Committee for Trade to Colonial Bank, 8 August 1838, BT 3/28.
17. Petition dated 22 November 1838, T 1/3473.
18. Normandy to MacGregor, 14 March 1839, CO 28/132.
19. Colonial Bank to Colonial Office, 16 January 1839, CO 318/143.
20. Law Officers to Colonial Office, 2 February 1839, CO 318/143.
21. Colonial Bank to Colonial Office, 12 February 1839, CO 318/143.
22. Colonial Bank to Colonial Office, 12 November 1840, BT 1/369.
23. Innes to Colonial Office, 19 February 1841, CO 318/151.
24. Committee for Trade to Colonial Office, 9 March 1841, CO 318/151.
25. Colonial Bank to Committee for Trade, 12 March 1841, BT 1/371.
26. Law Officers of the Crown to Committee for Trade, BT 1/372.
27. Derby to Robinson, circular of 29 April 1884, CO 854/25.
28. Telegrams of 14 and 21 January 1899, CO 318/296; Chamberlain to Hay, no. 80 of 12 May 1899, CO 28/251.
29. *Barbadian*, 4 December 1839; MacGregor to Russell, no. 10 of 29 January 1840, CO 28/133.
30. Deed no. 298, 18 January 1840, BA.
31. *Barbadian*, 29 April 1840.
32. 1 May 1840, UWI Library St Augustine, Trinidad, C 1840/3.
33. 2 November 1840, C 1840/32; 1 January 1841, C 1841/1; 16 August 1841, C1841/27.
34. Stanley to Grey, no. 65 of 12 May 1843, BA.
35. 1 November 1844, C 1844/46.
36. Stanley to Grey, no. 136 of 27 June 1845, BA.
37. Grey to Stanley, no. 58 of 6 September 1845, CO 28/162.
38. Gladstone to Grey, no. 1 of 30 December 1845, BA.

39. Grey to Reid, no. 15 of 6 March 1847, BA.
40. *Liberal*, 27 November 1847; *Barbadian*, 1 December 1847.
41. *Liberal*, 1 December 1847.
42. Ibid.
43. Extract from *Trinidad Gazette* dated 3 December 1847, *Barbadian*, 11 December 1847.
44. *Barbadian*, 1 December 1847.
45. Reid to Grey, no. 80 of 7 December 1847, CO 28/167.
46. *Liberal*, 2 February 1848.
47. Reid to Grey, no. 15 Financial of 26 February 1848, CO 28/168.
48. *Liberal*, 29 April 1848.
49. *Barbados Globe*, 28 February 1850.

CHAPTER 4

1. Kimberley to Rawson, circular of 27 June 1871, CO 854/12; circular of 1 February 1872, CO 854/13.
2. Kimberley to Rawson, 10 May 1872, CO 854/13.
3. Rawson to Kimberley, no. 30 of 9 March 1872, CO 28/216.
4. Kimberley to Rawson, circular of 18 July 1872, CO 854/13; Rawson to Kimberley, no. 93 of 28 August 1872, CO 28/216.
5. Hicks-Beach to Strahan, circular (no. 2) of 27 February 1879, CO 854/20.
6. Strahan to Hicks-Beach, no. 67 of 14 May 1880, CO 321/34.
7. Kimberley to Robinson, circular of 28 January 1881, CO 854/22; Holland to Lees, circulars of 13 August and 23 December 1887, CO 854/28; Lyttelton to Probyn, circular of 14 July 1905, CO 854/41; Crewe to Carter, circular of 11 November 1909, CO 854/45.
8. Milner to O'Brien, no. 213 of 15 November 1920, CO 318/359; O'Brien to Milner, no. 334 of 18 December 1920, CO 318/359.
9. Crown Agents to Colonial Office, 7 February 1934, T 160/672; Colonial Office to Crown Agents, 6 April 1934, T 160/672.
10. Harcourt to Probyn, Misc. of 8 May 1934, BA; Probyn to Harcourt, no. 106 of 8 June 1934, BA.
11. Carnarvon to Walker, circular of 30 November 1866, CO 854/8; Walker to Carnarvon, no. 564 of 9 February 1867, CO 28/204.
12. Knutsford to Hay, circular of 16 April 1892, CO 854/31.
13. O'Brien to Milner, no. 77 of 23 April 1919, CO 318/348; O'Brien to Milner, no. 193 of 30 July 1921, CO 28/299.

14. Carnarvon to Rawson, circular of 27 April 1874, CO 854/15; circular of 10 April 1876, CO 854/17.
15. Rawson to Carnarvon, no. 71 of 22 June 1874, CO 321/1.
16. Rawson to Carnarvon, no. 93 of 5 August 1874, CO 321/1; no. 112 of 22 September 1874, CO 321/1.
17. Holland to Lees, circular of 13 August 1887, CO 854/28.
18. Treasury to Colonial Office, 9 May 1889, CO 111/454; Colonial Office to Treasury, 16 May 1889, CO 111/454; Treasury to Colonial Office, 7 June 1889, CO 111/454.
19. Knutsford to Lees, no. 52 of 12 June 1889, CO 111/454; Lees to Knutsford, no. 118 of 30 June 1889, CO 28/226.
20. Treasury to Colonial Office, 22 July 1889, CO 111/454.
21. Treasury to Colonial Office, 18 August 1890, CO 318/280; Colonial Office to Treasury, 25 August 1890, CO 318/280.
22. Council Office to Treasury, 6 December 1890, CO 318/281; Treasury to Colonial Office, 23 April 1891, CO 318/281; Colonial Office to Treasury, 4 May 1891, CO 318/281.
23. Colonial Office to Mint, 9 September 1892, Mint 13/53.
24. Treasury to Colonial Office, 24 May 1915, CO 111/603; Harcourt to Probyn, no. 88 of 9 June 1915, CO 111/603.
25. Probyn to Law, no. 191 of 31 August 1915, CO 111/603.
26. 13 April 1916, CO 318/339; Treasury to Colonial Office, 13 April 1917, CO 111/614.
27. Minutes of the House of Assembly, 5, 12 and 26 March 1839, CO 31/54.
28. Reid to Grey, no. 8 of 17 January 1848, CO 28/168; Grey to Reid, no. 72 of 1 April 1848, CO 28/169.
29. Grey to Hincks, circular of 5 February 1852, CO 318/195.
30. Grey to Hincks, circular of 11 March 1852, Enclosure Letter of 29 January 1852, Colonial Bank to Treasury, CO 854/4.
31. Grey to Hincks, circular of 11 March 1852, Enclosure Letter of 20 February 1852, Treasury to Colonial Bank, CO 854/4.
32. Hamilton to Pakington, General (4) of 30 April 1852, CO 28/176.
33. Treasury Minutes, 12 October 1852.
34. Hincks to Lytton, no. 66 of 18 December 1858, CO 28/188.
35. Carnarvon to Hincks, circulars of 30 May and 31 August 1859, CO 854/6.
36. Hicks Beach to Dundas, circular of 9 November 1878, CO 854/19.
37. Dundas to Hicks Beach, 1 March 1879, CO 884/3.
38. Knutsford to Lees, no. 118 of 18 September 1888, CO 28/226.
39. Lees to Knutsford, no. 140 of 30 July 1889, CO 28/226.

40. Chamberlain to Hay, General of 22 February 1898, CO 501/5.
41. Chamberlain to Hay, conf. of 3 April 1900, CO 884/6.
42. Treasury to Colonial Office, 12 June 1902, CO 318/303.
43. Hodgson to Swettenham, 24 March 1904, T 1/9432.
44. Blake to Knutsford, no. 82 of 16 April 1891, CO 137/545; Knutsford to Blake, 29 May 1891, CO 137/545; Legislative Council Minutes of Jamaica, 18 February 1892, CO 137/545.
45. Minutes of 16 January 1900, CO 137/605.
46. Colonial Bank to Colonial Office, 19 January 1920, CO 318/362.
47. Amery to O'Brien, Misc. of 23 February 1920, BA.
48. Circulars nos. 113 of 13 October and 127 of 5 December 1946, CO 852/541/9; no. 48 of 16 February 1947, CO 852/679/2.
49. Treasury to Colonial Office, 21 October 1920, CO 318/359; Colonial Office to Treasury, 12 November 1920, CO 318/359.
50. Young to Thomas, no. 400 of 31 December 1935, CO 323/1349/2; Thomas to Young, no. 86 of 24 March 1936, CO 323/1349/2.
51. Thomas to Young, no. 107 of 29 April 1936, CO 323/1349/2.
52. Gore to Young, no. 195 of 11 August 1936, CO 323/1353/1.
53. Gore to Young, no. 161 of 21 June 1937, CO 323/1414/1; Young to Gore, no. 264 of 31 August 1937, CO 323/1414/1; Gore to Young, no. 249 of 29 September 1937, CO 323/1414/1.
54. Young to Gore, no. 67 of 25 February 1938, BA.
55. Stanley to Bushe, tel. no. 155 of 24 May 1943, CO 852/354/14.
56. Grey to Colebrooke, circular of 5 February 1852, CO 318/195.
57. Newcastle to Colebrooke, circular of 3 September 1853, CO 854/4; Newcastle to Colebrooke, circular of 13 March 1854, CO 854/4.
58. Newcastle to Walker, circular of 29 August 1863, CO 854/7; Walker to Newcastle, no. 196 of 27 October 1863, CO 28/197.
59. Carnarvon to Strahan, circular of 15 July 1876, CO 884/3; Hennessy to Carnarvon, no. 202 of 12 September 1876, CO 321/11.
60. Strahan to Hicks Beach, no. 50 of 2 May 1878, CO 321/19.
61. Hicks Beach to Strahan, circular of 15 November 1878, CO 854/19.
62. Colonial Bank to Colonial Office, 12 October 1907, CO 318/317.
63. Crewe to Carter, no. 162 of 9 December 1907, CO 318/317; Carter to Elgin, no. 7 of 11 January 1908, CO 318/317.
64. Crewe to Carter, no. 64 of 11 June 1908, CO 318/319.
65. Stubbs to Cunliffe-Lister, no. 205 of 10 May 1932, CO 323/1165/3.
66. Question and Answer in the House of Commons, 8 February, 1934 and 15 May 1935, T 160/609.

140 Notes to pages 71–81

67. Cunliffe-Lister to Newlands, no. 57 of 10 March 1933, CO 323/1165/3; Owen to Cunliffe-Lister, no. 136 of 16 May 1933, CO 323/1165/3; MacDonald to Young, no. 291 of 18 November 1935, CO 323/1165/3; Young to Thomas, no. 394 of 21 December 1935, CO 323/1314/6.
68. Hennessy to Carnarvon, no. 192 of 25 August 1876, CO 884/3.
69. May 1923, Mint 20/767.
70. Colonial Reports of Barbados, 1954 to 1961, HSMO.

CHAPTER 5

1. Probyn to Harcourt, no. 156 of 1 September 1914, CO 28/283; Harcourt to Probyn, No, 124 of 24 October 1914, CO 28/283; Probyn to Harcourt, no. 88 of 16 April 1915, CO 28/283.
2. Colonial Bank to Colonial Office, 31 December 1919, CO 318/352; O'Brien to Milner, no. 295 of 9 November 1920, CO 318/356; Treasury to Colonial Office, 11 February 1921, CO 318/356; Churchill to O'Brien, no. 44 of 21 February 1921, CO 318/367.
3. Royal Bank of Canada to Colonial Office, 21 December 1910, T 1/11325; Colonial Office to Treasury, 5 January 1911, T 1/11325.
4. Harcourt to Probyn, no. 27 of 28 February 1911, CO 28/277.
5. *Barbados Globe*, 8 March 1911.
6. Royal Bank of Canada to Colonial Secretary, Barbados, 21 March 1911 and 30 October 1911, BA.
7. Canadian Bank of Commerce to Colonial Office, 21 March 1921, CO 318/368.
8. Churchill to O'Brien, no. 169 of 12 July 1921, CO 501/7.
9. O'Brien to Churchill, no. 214 of 20 August 1921, CO 318/364; O'Brien to Churchill, no. 223 of 26 August 1921, CO 318/364.
10. Churchill to O'Brien, no. 224 of 20 September 1921, CO 318/369.
11. O'Brien to Churchill, no. 284 of 8 November 1921, CO 318/365.
12. 22 December 1921, Treasury to Colonial Office, CO 318/367.
13. Churchill to O'Brien, tel. of 29 December 1921, CO 318/367; Churchill to O'Brien, tel. no. 3 of 9 January 1922, CO 318/367.
14. Colonial Bank to Colonial Office, 22 February 1908, CO 318/319.
15. 4 March 1908, CO 318/319.
16. Colonial Office to Treasury, 1 April 1908, CO 318/319; Treasury to Colonial Office, 20 April 1908, CO 318/319.
17. Colonial Office to Colonial Bank, 4 May 1908, CO 318/319.

18. Colonial Bank to Colonial Office, 11 June 1908, CO 318/319.
19. Colonial Office to Treasury, 17 July 1908, CO 318/319; Treasury to Colonial Office, 4 August 1908, CO 318/319.
20. Crewe to Carter, conf. of 16 February 1909, CO 318/320; Carter to Crewe, conf. of 10 May 1909, CO 28/272.
21. Treasury to Colonial Office, 28 July 1909, CO 318/320; Colonial Office to Colonial Bank, 6 September 1909, CO 318/320; Colonial Bank to Colonial Office, 29 September 1909, CO 318/320.
22. CO 318/321.
23. Colonial Bank to Colonial Office, 21 March 1911, CO 318/327.
24. Colonial Office to Treasury, 2 January 1912, T 1/11383.
25. Harcourt to Probyn, conf. of 30 January 1912, CO 318/329; Baster, *Imperial Banks*, 36.
26. Treasury to Colonial Office, 8 June 1914, CO 318/333; Colonial Office to Treasury, 22 June 1914, T 1/11801.
27. Colonial Bank to Treasury, 19 February 1914, CO 318/333.
28. Colonial Bank to Colonial Office, 28 July 1915, CO 318/337.
29. Colonial Bank to Colonial Office, 6 October 1915, CO 318/337.
30. Treasury to Colonial Office, 26 October 1915, CO 318/335.
31. Colonial Office to Colonial Bank, 6 November 1915, CO 318/335; Treasury to Colonial Office, 7 December 1915, T 7/41.
32. Colonial Bank to Colonial Office, 22 February 1916, CO 318/340.
33. Board of Trade to Treasury, 12 April 1917, CO 318/343.
34. Milner to O'Brien, 15 July 1919, CO 318/348.
35. Treasury to Colonial Bank, 6 May 1913, CO 318/331.
36. Colonial Bank to Treasury, 10 July 1916, CO 318/339; Treasury to Colonial Bank, 12 August 1916, CO 318/339.
37. Treasury to Colonial Bank, 7 April 1917, T 1/12592.
38. Treasury to Colonial Bank, 10 October 1918, CO 318/347.
39. Colonial Bank to Treasury, 13 June 1919, CO 318/350.
40. Colonial Office to Treasury, 12 April 1917, CO 318/343.
41. Treasury to Colonial Bank, 13 November 1919, T 1/12592.
42. Colonial Bank to Treasury, 18 November 1919, CO 318/350; Treasury to Colonial Office, 29 November 1919, CO 318/350.
43. Treasury to Colonial Office, 29 November 1919, CO 318/350; Colonial Office to Treasury, 14 January 1920, CO 318/359.
44. Treasury to Colonial Office, 3 January 1920, CO 318/359.
45. Colonial Bank to Treasury, 25 May 1920, T 1/12592.

46. Manager, Royal Bank of Canada to Colonial Secretary, Barbados, 22 March 1919, BA; Milner to O'Brien, no. 47 of 3 April 1919, BA.
47. Royal Bank of Canada to Colonial Secretary, Barbados, 6 and 10 January 1920, BA.
48. Colonial Office to Treasury, 14 January 1920, CO 318/359; O'Brien to Milner, no. 19 of 28 January 1920, CO 28/297; Colonial Office to Royal Bank of Canada, 11 February 1920, T 1/12592.
49. Royal Bank of Canada to Colonial Office, 25 February 1920, CO 318/360.
50. Colonial Office to Treasury, 8 March 1920, T 1/12592.
51. Treasury to Colonial Office, 11 March 1920, T 1/12592; Colonial Office to Royal Bank of Canada, 20 March 1920, CO 318/359.
52. Royal Bank of Canada to Colonial Office, 22 March 1920, CO 318/360.
53. Colonial Office to Royal Bank of Canada, 29 June 1920, CO 318/354; Royal Bank of Canada to Colonial Office, 6 July 1920, CO 318/361; Colonial Office to Treasury, 23 July 1920, CO 318/361; Treasury to Colonial Office, 6 August 1920, CO 318/359.
54. Colonial Office to Royal Bank of Canada, 26 August 1920, CO 318/359.
55. O'Brien to Milner, conf. of 12 March 1920, CO 28/297.
56. Royal Bank of Canada to Colonial Office, 29 September 1920, CO 318/361.
57. Royal Bank of Canada to Colonial Office, 2 December 1920, CO 318/361.
58. Colonial Office to Treasury, 29 June 1920, CO 318/354; Treasury to Colonial Office, 6 August 1920, CO 318/359.
59. Milner to O'Brien, no. 157 of 27 August 1920, CO 318/359; O'Brien to Milner, no. 290 of 3 November 1920, CO 318/356.
60. Milner to O'Brien, no. 13 of 19 January 1921, CO 318/365; O'Brien to Churchill, no. 251 of 1 October 1921, CO 318/365.
61. Devonshire to O'Brien, no. 18 of 5 February 1923, CO 318/377.
62. O'Brien to Devonshire, no. 62 of 3 May 1923, CO 318/377.
63. Devonshire to O'Brien, no. 91 of 6 June 1923, CO 318/375; O'Brien to Devonshire, no. 158 of 7 September 1923, CO 318/375.
64. Thomas to O'Brien, no. 30 of 23 February 1924, CO 318/376.
65. Hay to Chamberlain, conf. no. 11 of 5 July 1900, CO 884/6.
66. Harcourt to Probyn, conf. of 2 January 1912, CO 318/327; Probyn to Harcourt, conf. of 28 March 1912, CO 28/278.
67. Probyn to Harcourt, no. 86 of 31 March 1913, CO 28/280.
68. Harcourt to Probyn, no. 82 of 19 May 1913, CO 28/280.
69. O'Brien to Milner, no. 295 of 9 November 1920, CO 318/356.

70. O'Brien to Milner, tel. of 10 December 1920, CO 318/356; Milner to O'Brien, tel. of 13 December 1920, CO 318/356; Milner to O'Brien, tel. of 8 January 1921, CO 318/356.
71. Young to Cunliffe-Lister, no. 107 of 28 May 1934, BA.
72. Young to Cunliffe-Lister, no. 218 of 25 September 1934, BA; Young to Cunliffe-Lister, no. 12 of 15 January 1935, BA.
73. Lloyd to Waddington, secret no. 142 of 9 August 1940, CO 852/284/6.
74. Governor, British Guiana to Governor, Barbados, 13 August 1940, BA.
75. Governor, Trinidad to Secretary of State repeated to Governors of Barbados and British Guiana, no. 581 of 23 August 1940, CO 852/284/6.
76. Waddington to Lloyd repeated to Two Governors, no. 210 of 3 September 1940, CO 852/284/6.
77. Beckett to Young, 19 November 1940, CO 852/284/6.
78. Governor, Trinidad to Secretary of State repeated to the Two Governors, tel. no. 15 of 5 January 1941, CO 852/284/6.
79. Accountant General, Trinidad to Colonial Secretary, Barbados, 30 March 1942, BA.
80. Creech Jones to Savage, no. 227 of 12 June 1950, CO 852/1061/2; Savage to Creech Jones, no. 329 of 15 July 1950, CO 852/1061/2.
81. MacDonald to Waddington, secret no. 14 of 21 September 1938, CO 852/157/7.
82. Chairman, Barclays Bank to MacDonald, 3 October 1938, CO 852/157/7.
83. Waddington to MacDonald, secret of 30 January 1939, CO 852/214/4.
84. Barclays Bank to Treasury, 4 January 1939, CO 852/214/8; Treasury to Barclays Bank, 5 January and 30 June 1939, CO 852/214/8.
85. Forrest to Grant, 4 June 1942, CO 852/359/2.
86. Lloyd to Waddington, secret no. 127 of 27 June 1940, CO 852/284/6.
87. Waddington to Lloyd, secret no.175 of 29 July 1940, CO 852/284/6.
88. Lloyd to Waddington, secret no. 142 of 9 August 1940, CO 852/284/6.
89. Moyne to Bushe, conf. no. 258 of 9 October 1941, CO 852/358/21.
90. Bushe to Moyne, no. 330 of 3 November 1941, CO 852/358/21.
91. Moyne to Bushe, no. 343 of 22 December 1941, CO 852/358/21.
92. Bushe to Cranborne, no. 72 of 28 February 1942, CO 852/358/22.
93. Cranborne to Bushe, no. 190 of 12 June 1942, CO 852/358/22; Bushe to Cranborne, no. 231 of 18 June 1942, CO 852/358/22.
94. Cranborne to Bushe, no. 394 of 14 November 1942, CO 852/359/2.
95. Bushe to Stanley, no. 7 of 4 January 1943, CO 852/359/2.
96. Stanley to Bushe, no. 73 of 3 March 1943, CO 852/354/17.

97. Stanley to Bushe, no. 12 of 15 January 1942, CO 852/359/2; Stanley to Bushe, no. 394 of 14 November 1942, CO 852/359/2; Stanley to Bushe, no. 9 of 8 January 1943, CO 852/359/2.
98. Moyne to Bushe, no. 39 of 5 February 1942, CO 852/359/2.
99. Stanley to Bushe, no. 144 of 17 May 1943, CO 852/359/3.
100. Stanley to Bushe, no. 356 of 4 December 1943, CO 852/359/3.
101. Stanley to Bushe, no. 169 of 3 June 1943, CO 852/359/2; Bushe to Stanley, no. 342 of 12 June 1943, CO 852/359/2.
102. Bank Notes (Amendment) Order of 22 June 1943; Proclamation of 20 November 1943; Proclamation of 11 December 1943; Stanley to Bushe, no. 194 of 31 May 1944, CO 852/534/3; Order of 22 June 1944; Order of 7 April 1945.

CHAPTER 6

1. Chamberlain to Hay, conf. of 3 April 1900, CO 884/6.
2. Hay to Chamberlain, conf. no. 11 of 5 July 1900, CO 884/6.
3. Treasury to Colonial Office, 12 June 1902, CO 318/303.
4. Colonial Office to Treasury, 9 December 1920, T 160/71.
5. Devonshire to O'Brien, no. 89 of 3 July 1923, CO 318/377.
6. O'Brien to Devonshire, no. 215 of 22 December 1923, BA; O'Brien to Thomas, no. 26 of 10 March 1924, BA.
7. Thomas to O'Brien, no. 16 of 5 November 1924, BA.
8. Amery to Robertson, no. 17 of 20 February 1928, CO 318/389/1.
9. Amery to Robertson, no. 51 of 27 May 1929, BA; Robertson to Passfield, no. 198 of 22 August 1929, BA.
10. Moyne to Bushe, conf. of 31 December 1942, CO 852/354/18.
11. Stanley to Bushe, nos. 165 and 166 of 8 December 1943, BA.
12. Stanley to Stanley, no. 53 of 26 May 1944, CO 852/534/3.
13. Bushe to Stanley, no. 68 of 13 July 1944, CO 852/534/3.
14. Stockdale to Caine, 26 January 1945, CO 852/534/4.
15. Jamaica Legislative Council Minutes, 9 January 1948, National Library of Jamaica.
16. Thomas to Blood, no. 99 of 7 October 1947, BA.
17. CO 852/679/3.
18. CO 852/674/4.
19. CO 852/1059/7.
20. Savage to Creech Jones, Savingram no. 557 of 25 November 1950, CO 852/1061/2; tel. no. 357 of 12 December 1950, CO 852/1061/2; Creech Jones to Savage, tels. no. 289 of 9 December and no. 301 of 22 December 1950, CO 852/1061/2.

21. Governor, British Guiana to Secretary of State, tel. no. 7 of 7 January 1951, CO 852/1061/2.
22. Savage to Creech Jones, no. 229 of 12 April 1951, CO 852/1061/2.
23. BCCB Report for 1951, CO 852/1060/3.
24. Governor, Trinidad to Secretary of State, 6 June 1952, CO 852/1060/4.
25. CO 852/1060/7.
26. Newton to McDavid, 13 December 1951, CO 852/1060/7.
27. McDavid to Hulland, 29 December 1951, CO 852/1060/7.
28. CO 852/1060/7.
29. Governor Jamaica to WICIR Governors, 27 August 1954, CO 1025/49.
30. Lennox Boyd to Arundell, circular 859/54 of 10 September 1954, CO 1025/80; Arundell to Lennox Boyd, no. 532 of 30 September 1954, CO 1025/51.
31. Lennox Boyd to Arundell, no. 504 of 6 December 1955, CO 1025/51.
32. Arundell to Boyd, no. 128 of 29 February 1956, CO 1025/51; Boyd to Arundell, no. 138 of 6 April 1956, CO 1025/51; Arundell to Boyd, no. 685 of 20 November 1956, CO 1025/51.
33. Lennox Boyd to Arundell, circular no. 840/56 of 7 August 1956, CO 1025/51; Lennox Boyd to Arundell, no. 67 of 4 February 1957, CO 1025/51.
34. CO 1025/189; DO 200/134
35. Minister of Finance of Trinidad and Tobago to Executive Commissioner, BCCB, 12 December 1964, CO 1025/192.
36. FCO 48/86.
37. Ryan to Chairman, Regional Council of Ministers, 20 May 1964, CO 1025/195.
38. FCO 48/71.
39. Prime Minister of Barbados to Premiers of Participating Governments, 8 June 1970, FCO 63/446.
40. SI no. 77 of 29 April 1972 and SI nos. 175 and 176 of 15 November 1973.

Selected Bibliography

A Banking Centenary: Barclays Bank (Dominion, Colonial and Overseas), 1836–1936. London: William Brendon and Sons, 1938.

Baster, A.S. *The Imperial Banks*. London, 1929.

Bayley, F.W.N. *Four Years' Residence in the West Indies, 1826–1829*. London: William Kidd, 1833.

Brown, Deryck R. *History of Money and Banking in Trinidad and Tobago from 1789 to 1989*. Trinidad: Paria, 1989.

Callender, Charles Victor. "The Development of the Capital Market Institutions of Jamaica". *Social and Economic Studies* 14, no. 3, suppl. (1965).

Chalmers, Lord Robert. *A History of Currency in the British Colonies*. London, 1893.

Greaves, Ida. "Money and Currency in Barbados". *Journal of the Barbados Museum and Historical Society*. 19, no. 4 (August 1952): 164–68; 20, no. 1 (November 1952): 3–19; 20, no. 2 (February 1953): 53–66.

Hall, Douglas. *Free Jamaica, 1838–1865: An Economic History*. New Haven: Yale University Press, 1959.

Hall, Richard. *Laws of Barbados*. London, 1764.

Hinds, Allister. "Currency Unification in the British Caribbean, 1922–51". In *Before and After 1865*, edited by Brian Moore and Swithin Wilmot, 216–25. Kingston: Ian Randle, 1998.

Ligon, Richard. *A True and Exact History of the Island of Barbados*. London, 1657.

Lobdell, Richard A. "Patterns of Investment and Sources of Credit in the British West Indian Sugar Industry, 1838–1897", *Journal of Caribbean History* 4 (May 1972): 32–53.

Monteith, Kathleen. "Local Pressure versus Metropolitan Policy: The Clash over Banking Policy in the West Indies, 1939–43". In *Before and After 1865*, edited by Brian Moore and Swithin Wilmot, 226–35. Kingston: Ian Randle, 1998.

Moore, Samuel. *Laws of Barbados, 1762–1800*. London: Luke Hansard, 1801.

Nettles, Curtis P. *The Money Supply of the American Colonies before 1720*. Clifton, NJ: Augustus Kelly Publishers, 1973.

Pennington, James. *The Currency of the British Colonies*. London, 1848.
Poyer, John. *A History of Barbados from the First Discovery of the Island in the Year 1605 till the Accession of Lord Seaforth, 1801*. London, 1808.
Ragatz, L.J. *The Fall of the Planter Class in the British Caribbean, 1763 to 1833*. New York: Octagon, 1977.
Republic Bank Ltd. *From Colonial to Republic: 150 Years of Business and Banking in Trinidad and Tobago, 1837–1987*. Trinidad: Paria, 1987.
Schomburgh, R.H. *A History of Barbados*. London, 1847.
Shannon, H.A. "Evolution of Colonial Sterling Exchange Standard". *IMF Staff Papers* 1 (1950–51).
Thomas, C.Y. "Monetary and Financial Arrangements in a Dependent Monetary Economy". *Social and Economic Studies* 14, no. 4, suppl. (1965).
Worrell, DeLisle, ed. *The Economy of Barbados, 1946–1980*. Central Bank of Barbados, 1982.

Index

Act No. 20 (1920, Barbados), 67
agriculture
   external finance in development of, 1–2, 39
Alleyne, Sir Reynold
   objections to 1838 proclamation, 33–34
American colonies
   paper bills of credit, 8–9, 11
   as trading partner, 2, 27
   See also United States
anchor money, 18–19, 27–28
apprenticeship system
   abolition of, 34
   cash payments, and scarcity of coins, 27–28, 29, 30
   coin denominations used, 24, 25
Associated West Indies Chambers of Commerce
   proposals for currency unification, 107–8

Bahamas, displacement of British silver coins, 69
balance of trade
   with American traders, 27
   and currency unification, 103
   between England and colonial planters, 1–2
Bank Circulation Redemption Fund, 77
Bank Notes (Amendment) Act No. 13 (1943), 99
Bank of British Guiana, 76, 83
Bank of England notes, 96–98
   repatriation of surplus coins, 97–98
Bank of Jamaica, 76
Bank of Nova Scotia, 65, 76, 85
   and Colonial Bank, 80
   note issues, restriction of, 98–99
   notes, issuance of in Jamaica, 103
   request for coins, 66
banks and banking companies
   bank notes as legal tender, 75–76
   Bank of British Guiana, 76, 83
   Bank of Jamaica, 76
   banking regulations, 127–30
   Canadian banks. *See* Canadian banks
   circulation of government currency notes, 99, 100–101t
   excess note issues, 85–88
   foreign bank restrictions, 85
   National City Bank of New York, 85
   notes, issuance of, 39, 76
   Planters' Bank, 76
   regulations governing, 38–39
   Royal Bank of Liverpool, 50–51, 54
   shareholders liability, 39
   See also Colonial Bank; West India Bank

149

Index

Barbadian (newspaper) on proclamation of 1838, 35
Barbados, 28–29
  1825 proclamation, 19–25, 31
  Act No. 20 (1920), 67
  anchor money, 18–19, 27–28
  applications for coin, 56–57
  Bank Notes Act No. 5 (1911), 78, 79
  BCCB notes in circulation, 118
  BCCB participation, 109, 112
  British Guiana and West Indies groats, 60–61
  Canadian Bank of Commerce, 78–80
  Central Bank note denominations, 123
  Central Bank of Barbados Act No. 6 (1970), 123
  coins current (1826–1829), 22
  coins current in 1815, 17
  coins in circulation, 71
  Colonial Bank, 41–42
  Commissioners of Trade and Plantations, 8
  commodities as payment system, 2–3, 16
  comparative scale of value (1825), 20–21
  currency, and the Coinage Act, 60
  currency unification congress, 107–8
  Demonetization Act No. 4 (1879), 70
  distribution of interest on excess notes, 88–89
  dollar, proposal for adoption of, 27
  early currency system, 1–15
  East Caribbean Currency Authority, 119–24
  gold coins in circulation, 56
  Government Currency Notes (Barbados) Act No. 12, 91–93
  Government Currency Notes Bill, 68
  government currency notes issued, 94, 95
  imports and exports of coins, notes and bullion, 71–74
  independent status of, 121–23
  notes in circulation, 123–24
  Paper Credit Act (1706), 8
  public debt (1722), 9
  reciprocal legal tender of government notes, 93–95
  Royal Bank of Canada, 77–78
  scarcity of coins, 27–31
  Stamp Act No. 3 (1916), 86
  state of currency (1700–1739), 9–11
  surplus of British silver coins, 67–68
  withdrawal from West Indies (Associated States) Council of Ministers, 122–23
Barbados Agricultural Aids Act, 80
Barbados Bank, 46–47
Barbados Bank Notes Reserve Fund, 78
Barbados Currency Act No. 31 (1950), 110–11
Barbados Currency Board, 94
Barclays Bank (DC&O)
  and Board of Commissioners of Currency, British Caribbean Territories (Eastern Group), 111, 112
  circulation of government currency notes, 100–101t
  note issues, restriction of, 98–99
  notes, issuance of in Second World War, 96
  and reconstitution of Colonial Bank, 80, 83–85
  See also Colonial Bank
Barton, Irlam and Higginson, 50–51, 54
Bayley, F.N.
  Four Years' Residence in the West Indies, 1826–1829, 22

Beckles, J.A., 30
Beckwith, Governor, request for coins, 16–17
Board of Commissioners of Currency, British Caribbean Territories (Eastern Group)
  Barbados Currency Act No. 31 (1950), 110–11
  Closer Association of the British West Indian Colonies conference, 108–9
  Coin Continuation Board, 117, 120–21
  coins issued, 113
  commissioners, 112
  currency denominations, 112
  Currency Fund Income Account, 110
  Currency Surplus Account, 110, 117
  draft legislation defining, 110
  East Caribbean Currency Authority, 117
  "Establishment of a Central Authority to Control West Indian Currency", 105–7
  notes in circulation, Barbados, 118
  "Notice of Replacement", 116–17
  prepatory committee meetings, 109–11
Bovell, John, 30–31
Bradbury notes, 76
Britain
  anchor money, 18–19, 27–28
  assimilation of Barbadian currency, 37
  British Coinage Act (1946), 67
  Coinage Act (1870), 58
  coins current in United Kingdom (1845), 26–27
  Colonial Branch Mint Act (1866), 57–58
  colonial currency policy, 1–15
  Export and Import Duty Act, 37
  government currency notes, 75–76
  imports and exports of coins, notes and bullion, 71–74
  proclamation of 1825, 19–25, 31
  redemption and repatriation of coins, 117
  Silver Coinage Act (1920), 67
  sterling devaluation, 121
  United Kingdom Coinage Acts, 65
  West Indian request for coins, 16–17
British Coinage Act (1946), 67
British Guiana
  1853–54 values of US gold coins, 69
  1854 values of US gold coins, 69
  BCCB participation, 109, 112
  British Guiana and West Indies groats, 59–61
  currency unification congress, 107–8
  distribution of interest on excess notes, 88–89
  export of anchor coins to, 27–28
  external finance in, 39
  government currency notes, 89–93
  government currency notes, circulation of, 94, 95
  reciprocal legal tender of government notes, 93–95
  and Royal Bank of Canada, 83
  seignorage on groats, 60–61
British sterling
  1651 values, 4–5
  1704–7 values, 6–7
  1791 values of gold coins, 13–14
  1819 values, 18
  1825 comparative scale of value, 20–21
  1825 proclamation, 19–25, 31
  1831 Mint regulations, 25–27
  1834 values, 23–25
  1836, island currency value on, 27–31

British sterling *(continued)*
  1836 values, 28, 29
  branch mints, 57–58
  bronze coins, 58
  circulation of in Second World War, 96–98
  conversion formula, 22
  copper coins, 18, 30, 58
  as current money, 3
  debased and mutilated coins, 11–15
  denominational currency, 1
  devaluation of, 121
  export of, 28–29
  parity with Spanish dollar, 31
  silver coins as legal tender, 61–65
  silver coins, demand and supply of, 59–61
  silver content of coins, 67
  sovereigns as legal tender, 23–25
  surplus of British silver coins, 67–68
British West Indian dollars
  circulation of in Barbados, 118, 123–24
  exports of sugar and molasses, 126
  imports and exports, value of, 125
  issued, 95
bronze coins, 58

Canadian Bank Act(s), 77
Canadian Bank of Commerce, 78–80
  circulation of government currency notes, 100–101t
  note issues, restriction of, 98–99
Canadian banks
  Bank Circulation Redemption Fund, 77
  Bank of Nova Scotia, 65, 66, 80, 85, 98–99, 103
  Canadian Bank of Commerce, 78–80, 98–99, 100–101
  Canadian banking legislation, 77
  Central Gold Reserve, 87
  excess note issues, 86–87, 88
  interest paid on notes, 86–87
  note issues, restriction of, 98–99
  notes, issuance of, 76, 79–80
  Royal Bank of Canada, 77–78
  security deposits required of, 80
  Union Bank of Halifax, 65, 76
Carnarvon, Earl of, 63
Clarke, Robert B., 30
Closer Association of the British West Indian Colonies
  recommendations for currency unification, 108–9
Coin Continuation Board, 117, 120–21
Coinage Act (1870), 58
Colonial Bank, 39–46
  and 1838 proclamation, 33–34
  acceptable transactions, 40
  applications for coin, 56
  Bank Notes Act No. 5 (1911), 78
  bank notes as legal tender, 75–76
  as Barclays Bank (DC&O), 85
  charter violation, 44
  circulation of government currency notes, 100–101t
  Colonial Bank Tokens, 41
  competition with West India Bank, 47–48
  Cuban rumour, 43–44
  demonetization of silver dollars, 70
  dividends paid, 53
  and failure of West India Bank, 50–51
  incorporation of by royal charter, 40
  inter-island drafts, 81–82
  and island currency, 29–30
  note redemption, 81–83
  notes, issuance of, 40, 45, 46, 84

notes of in payment of customs duties, 42–43
objections to limited tender of British silver, 62–65
as obstructive institution, 80–82
reconstitution of, 83–85
request for coins, 40–41, 66
shareholders liability, 40
supplementary charter, 43
supply of currency to West Indies, 36–37
terms of business, 41–42, 45
See also Barclays Bank (DC&O)
Colonial Bank Act (1898), 45–46, 80
Colonial Bank Act (1900), 81, 85
Colonial Bank Act (1916), 84
Colonial Bank Act (1917), 84
Colonial Bank Act (1925), 84
Colonial Branch Mint Act (1866), 57–58
Colonial Office
  notes, issuance of, 78–80
  proposals for currency unification, 102–5
  regulation of notes by Canadian banks, 76, 77–78
  review of currency administration, 113–14
  wartime policy, 98–99
colonial policy
  external finance in development of agriculture, 1–2
Columbian coins
  1838 values, 32–37, 69
Commissioners of Trade and Plantations
  Paper Credit Act (1706) and, 8
Committee for Trade
  special colonial coins, 17
commodities as payment system, 2–3
Companies Act (1862), 83

Cools-Lartigue, L., 112
copper coins
  1819 exchange rate, 18
  1831 Mint regulations, 25–27
  export of, 14–15
  as legal tender, 20, 58
  use of in West Indies, 14, 17–18, 24–25
cotton, as commodity in payment system, 2–3
Cuke, H.A., 109, 112
cupro-nickel coinage, 67
currency
  anchor money, 18–19, 27–28
  Coinage Act (1870), 58
  coins current in Barbados (1815), 17
  Colonial Branch Mint Act (1866), 57–58
  commodities as payment system, 2–3
  counterfeit coins, 11
  current money as standard in legislation, 3–5
  paper bills of credit, 7–11
  review of (1700–1739), 9–11
  shortages of in early currency system, 4–5, 7, 16
  withdrawal of worn coin from circulation, 55–57
  See also coins by country of origin
Currency Acts, amendments to, 114
Currency Fund Income Account, 110
currency legislation, early colonial system, 3–5
Currency Note Income Account, 92
Currency Note Law (1904), 67
Currency Notes (Reciprocal Legal Tender) Act (1937), 113
Currency Notes (Reciprocal Legal Tender) Act No. 1 (1941), 94

Currency of the British Colonies (Pennington), 7
Currency Surplus Account, 110
fund distribution, 117
currency unification
  Associated West Indies Chambers of Commerce proposals, 107–8
  background, 102–5
  Board of Commissioners of Currency, British Caribbean Territories (Eastern Group), 105–17
  Closer Association of the British West Indian Colonies, 108–9
  Currency Acts, amendments to, 114
  East Caribbean Currency Authority, 119–24
  "Establishment of a Central Authority to Control West Indian Currency", 105–7
  Ormsby-Gore Report, 103–4
  Regional Currency Board proposal, 107

Demonetization Act No. 4 (1879, Barbados), 70
denominational currency, 1
Disraeli, Benjamin, 63
dollars
  1838 values, 32–37
  British West Indian dollars issued, 95
  demonetization of silver dollars, 63, 70
  and island currency, 37
  proposal for adoption of, 27
  Public Accounts Act No. 1 (1949), 93
Dos Santos, A.P., 109
Dottin, Mr, on state of currency in Barbados (1700–1739), 9–11
doubloons, valuing of, 17–18, 23–24, 31, 32–37
  demonetization of, 70–71
Dutch coins, 1651 values, 4

East Caribbean Currency Authority, 117, 119–24
  Coin Continuation Board, 117, 120–21
  directors, 120
  note denominations, 120
  objectives of, 119–20
  Sterling Area Agreement, 121
Emancipation Act (1833), 39
English coins. *See* British sterling
English Sugar Duties Act, 54
"Establishment of a Central Authority to Control West Indian Currency", 105–7
Export and Import Duty Act, 37
Exportation of Money (Prohibition) Act No. 20 (1920), 88

Farquharson, C.S., 66
Federation of the West Indies
  Trinidad and Tobago independence, 114–16
fees and fines
  rating of in commodities, 2–3
  rating of in current money, 3
First World War
  bank notes as legal tender, 75–76
Foreign Banks Licensing Act (1920), 85
foreign coin
  1651 values, 4–5
  1704–7 values, 6–7
  1791 values of gold coins, 13–14
  1838 values, 32–37
  1853 values of US gold coins, 69
  1876 values, 70
  counterfeit coins, 11
  debased and mutilated coins, 11–15

light money, 10
US currency as legal tender, 71
valuation of, 37
Four Years' Residence in the West Indies, 1826–1829 (Bayley), 22
French coins
1651 values, 4
1704–7 values, 6–7
1791 values of gold coins, 13–14
silver coins, 10

gold, as sole standard of value, 19
gold coins
1651 values, 4–5
1704–7 values, 6–7
1791 values, 13–14
1831 Mint regulations, 25–27
1853–54 values of US gold coins, 69
army rate on, 22
branch mints, 57–58
circulation of in Barbados, 56
debased coins as light money, 10
disparity of assigned rates, 9
English sovereigns as legal tender, 23–25
new dollars vs. Spanish dollars, 23
proposal for US gold as legal currency, 62
government currency notes, 89–93
Bank of England notes, 96–98
circulation of, 99, 100–101t
currency reserves in Second World War, 96–98
reciprocal legal tender of, 93–95
redemption commissions, 98–99
restriction of, 98–99
Government Currency Notes Act (1937), 113
Government Currency Notes Bill, 68, 76
Grenada, BCCB participation, 117

Hall, Richard, 4
Holder, John, 8
Holtz, N., 112
House of Higginson and Co., failure of, 50–51

Innes, John, 44
inter-island drafts, 81–82
International Monetary Fund, 122

Jamaica
applications for coin, 56–57
BCCB participation, 109, 112–13
Canadian Bank of Commerce, 78–80
coins minted for, 25
Currency Note Law (1904), 67
currency unification congress, 107–8
excess note issues, 86–87
government currency notes, 89–93
notes, issuance of, 103
Royal Bank of Canada, 78
Jamaica Bank Notes Law No. 20 (1904), 77
Jamaica Bank Notes Legal Tender Law, 76
James I
proclamation on export of gold and silver, 1
Jordan, G.W., 17

Kendal, James, 3

Leeward Islands
BCCB participation, 112
British Guiana and West Indies groats, 60–61
currency, and the Coinage Act, 60
currency unification congress, 107–8
government currency notes, 90
reciprocal legal tender of government notes, 94

156 Index

legislation
  Act No. 20 (1920, Barbados), 67
  Bank Notes Act No. 5 (1911), 78, 79
  Bank Notes (Amendment) Act No. 13 (1943), 99
  Barbados Bank Notes Reserve Fund, 78
  Barbados Currency Act No. 31 (1950), 110–11
  Canadian Bank Act(s), 77
  Coinage Act (1870), 60
  Colonial Bank Act (1898), 45–46, 80
  Colonial Bank Act (1900), 81, 85
  Colonial Bank Act (1916), 84
  Colonial Bank Act (1917), 84
  Colonial Bank Act (1925), 84
  Companies Act (1862), 83
  Currency Notes (Reciprocal Legal Tender) Act (1937), 113
  Currency Notes (Reciprocal Legal Tender) Act No. 1 (1941), 94
  current money as standard in legislation, 3–5
  English Sugar Duties Act, 54
  Export and Import Duty Act, 37
  Exportation of Money (Prohibition) Act No. 20 (1920), 88
  Foreign Banks Licensing Act (1920), 85
  Government Currency Notes Act (1937), 113
  Government Currency Notes Bill, 68, 76
  Jamaica Bank Notes Law No. 20 (1904), 77
  Jamaica Bank Notes Legal Tender Law, 76
  Public Accounts Act No. 1 (1949), 93
  Stamp Act No. 3 (1916), 86
  Straits Settlement Ordinance (1938), 109

Liberal newspaper, criticism of Colonial Bank, 30
light money, 10

MacGregor, Sir Evan, 29
Martinique, export of copper coins to, 14–15
McDavid, E.F., 109–10, 112
M'Chlery, Michael
  Colonial Bank in Barbados, 41–42
merchants
  objections to 1838 proclamation, 32–34
  opposition to 1834 currency revaluing, 25
Mercury newspaper, support of Colonial Bank, 30
Mexican coins
  1651 values, 4–5
  1704–7 values, 6–7
  1838 values, 32–37, 69
  1876 values, 70
mints
  branch mints, 57–58
  closure of South American mints, 19–20
  proposals for colonial establishment, 5
Moore, Samuel, 4

National City Bank of New York, 85
Note Security Fund, 92, 114
notes, issuance of
  and Board of Commissioners of Currency, British Caribbean Territories (Eastern Group), 112
  Canadian banks, 76, 78–80
  Colonial Bank, 39, 40, 45, 46, 78–80
  Currency Note Income Account, 92
  distribution of interest on excess notes, 88–89

excess note issues, 85–88
Exportation of Money (Prohibition)
  Act No. 20 (1920), 88
government currency notes, 89–93
Note Guarantee Fund, 90
note redemption, 81–83
Note Security Fund, 92
Union Bank of Halifax, 65
West India Bank, 49–50

Ommanney, Sir M., 80
Ormsby-Gore, W., 103–4
Ormsby-Gore Report, 103–4

paper bills of credit
  economic effect of Queen Anne's
    proclamation, 7–11
  issuance of by American colonies, 8–9
  review of (1700–1739), 9–11
Paper Credit Act (1706), 8
Paper Credit Bill, 8
Peel, Sir Robert, 38
Pennington, James
  Currency of the British Colonies, 7
Percival, E., 78
Peru coins
  1704–7 values, 6–7
pieces of eight
  1651 values, 4–5
  1704–7 values, 6–7
planters
  and 1838 proclamation, 32–34
  Barbados Agricultural Aids Act, 80
  British merchants as factors, 16
  cash payments, and scarcity of coins,
    28, 29, 30
  credit availability, 79, 80
  dependence on West India Bank
    credit, 49–50
  external finance in development of

agriculture, 1–2, 39
  opposition to 1834 currency revalu-
    ing, 25
  request for coins, 25
Planters' Bank, 76
Portuguese coins
  1651 values, 4
  1791 values of gold coins, 13–14
Privy Council
  committee for coin, 32
  Paper Credit Act (1706) and, 8
  request for coins, 40–41
proclamation of 1791
  values of foreign coins, 13–14
proclamation of 1825
  introduction of British coins in
    colonies, 19–25, 27–31
proclamation of 1836
  island currency value in British silver,
    27–31
proclamation of 1838
  island currency values, 32–37
  new coinage issued, 26–27
  objections to, 32–34
proclamation of James I
  on export of gold and silver, 1
proclamation of Queen Anne
  and Act of 1707, 6–7
Public Accounts Act No. 1 (1949)
  accounts in dollars and cents, 93

Queen Anne, and Act of 1707, 6–7

Regional Currency Board, 107
Robertson, A.R.W., 112
Royal African Company, 8
Royal Bank of Canada
  acquisition of Bank of British Guiana,
    83
  bank notes as legal tender, 75–76

Royal Bank of Canada *(continued)*
  circulation of government currency notes, 100–101t
  Colonial Bank negotiations, 83, 90
  excess note issues, 86–87, 88
  note issues, restriction of, 98–99
  notes, issuance of, 79
  West Indies branches, 77–78
Royal Bank of Liverpool
  effect of failure on West India Bank, 50–51, 54
royal charters
  evolution of banking regulations, 38–39
Royal Mint
  1704–7 values of foreign coins, 6–7
  1831 regulations, 25–27
  anchor money, 18–19, 27–28
  assay of new dollars, 23
  branch mints, 57–58
  copper coins, minting of, 17
  expense responsibilities of colonial governments, 55–57
  process for procuring coins, 26–27
  recoinage of debased coins, 19
  redemption and repatriation of coins, 56, 67–68, 117
  seignorage, 19, 60–61, 66
Russell, Lord John, 39
Ryan, A.L., 119

Second World War
  currency reserves, 96–98
  defence regulations, 93
  US bases in Trinidad, 94
seignorage, 19, 60–61, 66
Sharpe, William, 8
Silver Coinage Act (1920), 67
  silver coins
  1651 values, 4–5

1704–7 values, 6–7
1825 values of, 21–22
1831 Mint regulations, 25–27
anchor money, 18–19, 27–28
clipped coins, as legal tender, 15
debased coins as light money, 10
demand and supply of, 59–61
demand for in England, 25
disparity of assigned rates, 9
groats, 59–61
legal tender of, 61–65
recoinage of, 19
scarcity of, 61
silver content of British coins, 67
surplus of British silver coins, 67–68
as tokens, 19
Treasury regulations for, 55–57
Spain
  South American mints, closure of, 19–20, 23
Spanish coins
  1651 values, 4–5
  1704–7 values, 6–7
  1791 values of gold coins, 13–14
  1825 values of, 20, 21–22
  1838 values, 32–37, 69
  as denominational currency, 1
  doubloons, scarcity of, 23–24
  doubloons, valuing of, 31
  gold coins, 10
  Spanish dollar, overvaluing of, 31
Spence, Louis, 109, 112
Spiers, D.W., 120
St Lucia
  limit on legal tender of British silver, 64–65
Straits Settlement Ordinance (1938), 109
Strathie, Sir Norman, 109
sugar, as commodity in payment system, 2–3

sugar industry
  English Sugar Duties Act, 54
  exports of sugar and molasses, 126
  external finance in development of, 39
  limit on legal tender of British silver, 64
  and West India Bank, 48–49

Thompson, E.A., 112
tobacco, as commodity in payment system, 2–3
Treasury
  antagonism with Colonial Office, 76
  Bradbury notes, 76
  Colonial Bank notes in payment of customs duties, 42–43
  excess note issues, 85–88
  government currency notes, 89–93
  proposals for currency unification, 103
  and reconstitution of Colonial Bank, 83–85
  repatriation of surplus coins, 67–68
  request for coins, 40–41
  responsibility for colonial banking charters, 39
  seignorage, 19, 66
  silver coins, regulations for supply of, 55–57
Trinidad and Tobago
  BCCB participation, 109, 112
  British Guiana and West Indies groats, 60–61
  Canadian Bank of Commerce, 78–80
  Central Bank Act (1964), 116
  currency unification congress, 107–8
  demonetization of doubloons, 70–71
  distribution of interest on excess notes, 88–89
  external finance in, 39
  government currency notes, 89–93, 94, 95
  independent status of, 114–16
  National City Bank of New York, 85
  notes, issuance of, 103
  reciprocal legal tender of government notes, 93–95
  Royal Bank of Canada, 78
  US bases in, 94, 97
troop payments
  anchor money, 19, 27–28
  army rate on foreign gold coins, 22
  in British coins, 20, 21
  copper coins, 18

Union Bank of Halifax, 76
  and Colonial Bank, 80
  notes, issuance of, 65, 103
United Kingdom. *See* Britain
United Kingdom Coinage Acts, 65
United States
  1853–54 values of US gold coins, 69
  bases in Trinidad in Second World War, 94, 97
  currency as legal tender, 71
  as trading partner, 16
  US dollar as basis for monetary system, 88
  US gold as legal currency, proposal for, 62
  See also American colonies

Walker, Alexander, 8
West India Bank, 46–54
  branch mismanagement, 52, 54
  branches of, 47
  capitalization of, 47–48, 54
  charter negotiations, 49

West India Bank *(continued)*
  Committee of Inspection report, 51–53, 54
  competition with Colonial Bank, 47–48
  dividends paid, 53
  failure of Royal Bank of Liverpool, 50–51, 54
  financial position, 51–52
  interest paid, 48
  notes, issuance of, 49–50
  and sugar industry, 48–49
West Indian Currency Board, 103
West Indies
  anchor money, 18–19, 27–28
  Board of Commissioners of Currency, British Caribbean Territories (Eastern Group), 105–17
  British Guiana and West Indies groats, 59–61
  copper coins, use of, 14
  currency unification, 102–17
  distribution of interest on excess notes, 88–89
  East Caribbean Currency Authority, 117, 119–24
  introduction of British coins, 23–25
  money of account, differences in, 35–37
  request for coins, 16–17
  scarcity of coins, 27–31
  seignorage, 19, 66
  silver coins, demand and supply of, 59–61
  US currency as legal tender, 71
West Indies (Associated States) Council of Ministers
  and Barbados independence, 121–23
West Indies Conferences
  currency unification resolutions, 104–5
Whitla, Mr, 30, 35
Windward Islands
  BCCB participation, 112
  British Guiana and West Indies groats, 60–61
  currency unification congress, 107–8
  government currency notes, 90
  reciprocal legal tender of government notes, 94
Woodbridge, Dudley, 7–8

www.ingramcontent.com/pod-product-compliance
Lightning Source LLC
Chambersburg PA
CBHW021844220426
43663CB00005B/388